Invitality

Easily Evangelize
By Inviting People Into Your Life, Your Church, and Into Christ

Dr. Adam Hirschy

Copyright © 2019 by Adam Hirschy

Invitality: Easily Evangelize By Inviting People Into Your Life, Your Church, And Into Christ

All rights reserved. No part of this publication may be reproduced, distributed or transmitted in any form or by any means, including photocopying, recording, or other electronic or mechanical methods, without the prior written permission of the publisher, except in the case of brief quotations embodied in critical reviews and certain other noncommercial uses permitted by copyright law.

Although the author and publisher have made every effort to ensure that the information in this book was correct at press time, the author and publisher do not assume and hereby disclaim any liability to any party for any loss, damage, or disruption caused by errors or omissions, whether such errors or omissions result from negligence, accident, or any other cause.

Adherence to all applicable laws and regulations, including international, federal, state and local governing professional licensing, business practices, advertising, and all other aspects of doing business in the US, Canada or any other jurisdiction is the sole responsibility of the reader and consumer.

Neither the author nor the publisher assumes any responsibility or liability whatsoever on behalf of the consumer or reader of this material. Any per-ceived slight of any individual or organization is purely unintentional.

The resources in this book are provided for informational purposes only and should not be used to replace the specialized training and professional judgment of a health care or mental health care professional.

Neither the author nor the publisher can be held responsible for the use of the information provided within this book. Please always consult a trained professional before making any decision regarding treatment of yourself or others.

Scriptures in the book were from the following:

Scripture taken from the New King James Version. Copyright © 1979, 1980, 1982 by Thomas Nelson, Inc. Used by permission. All rights reserved.

Scripture taken from the Amplified Bible, Copyright © 1954, 1958, 1962, 1964, 1965, 1987 by The Lockman Foundation. Used by permission.

Scripture quotations taken from the Holy Bible, New Living Translation, Copyright © 1996, 2004. Used by permission of Tyndale House Publishers, Inc. Wheaton, Illinois 60189. All rights reserved.

All scripture quotations in the publication are from The Message. Copyright © by Eugene H. Peterson 1993, 1994, 1995, 1996, 2000, 2001, 2002. Used by permission of NavPress Publishing Group.

ISBN-13: 978-0-578-55441-9
Library of Congress Control Number: 2019912330
Printed in the United States Of America

Download the free _Invitality_ Transformation Guide

Go to: http://bit.ly/2zufQLF

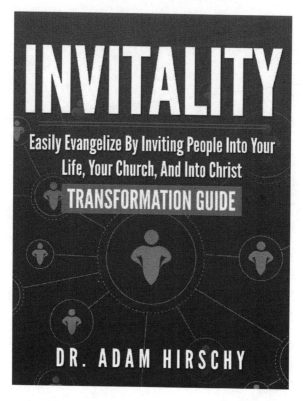

The *Invitality* Transformation Guide is a fast-start personal and small group life-change experience! You will grow spiritually and maximize results! When you download, you will enjoy full access to the *Invitality* community. The *Invitality* community is a group of world-changers sharing experiences, asking questions, praying, and encouraging one another!

Dedication

This book is dedicated to my Lord Jesus, my wife Heidi, and our children; for all of the encouragement, prayer, faith, and mutual dedication to the call of God upon our lives.

Special honor is given to the ministry partners who believed in the message and gave in order to make this dream a reality; may your reward in heaven be substantially greater than your reward on earth.

Invitation + Vitality= *Invitality*

Invitality: A personal and purposeful life culture of compelling invitation: inviting people into your life, inviting people into church, and inviting people to Christ.

Invitation: A request to be present or participate, incentive, inducement

Vitality: The peculiarity distinguishing the living from the nonliving, capacity to live and develop; power of enduring, lively and animated character

(Merriam-Webster, 2013)

Table of Contents

Dedication v
Foreword xi
Introduction xiii

Chapter One: Compelled 1
Chapter Two: The Power of *Invitality* 9
Chapter Three: True Worship 19
Chapter Four: Culture Shift 31
Chapter Five: Powerful Prayer for People 47
Chapter Six: Preach what Jesus Preached 59
Chapter Seven: Where's Your Fishing Hole? 69
Chapter Eight: *Invitality* = Church Growth 83
Chapter Nine: Practically Speaking 103
Chapter Ten: Tactful—Not Tacky 123
Chapter Eleven: Invitality Empowerment 139

Prayers that rock your world! 155
Bibliography 159

Foreword

Having pastored the same church for nearly thirty years, I have had the privilege of experiencing stages and stalls in growth and ministry. There is a core group of people in this church that has believed for years that God had more for us—that He's seen more *of* us than what we had experienced. It hasn't always been easy to hang on to that hope. But this is a group of people who love God, love people, and want to do God's will. They want to be a life-giving church. Together, we have endured dog days and doldrums, and now we have also been blessed to enjoy times of great momentum, seasons of successive, successful results. There is a practically palpable buzz of high morale and expectation.

God has used the word that Dr. Hirschy communicates in this book to help change the trajectory of this church. The vitality of the church has been converted into an attraction resulting in new guests every weekend. The boost brought to us has come through life lived on purpose. It's just as He writes: "Invitality is not a lifestyle of pushiness, but it is a lifestyle lived on purpose. It is purposely being unselfish with the goodness of God."

I immediately incorporated the message into our Sunday morning ministry programming. We have been the first to taste the fruit of this message—to see and enjoy the glorious changes it brings—but we are merely the first.

With gladness and anticipation, I urge you to receive this message and develop a lifestyle of *Invitality*. Thank God for His wonderful gifts!

—Loren Hirschy, Senior Pastor,
Word of Life Church, Iowa

Introduction

Are you really feeling Jesus's compassion for people far from God? Is your personal evangelism lifeless and your church stagnate? Are you laying up treasure in heaven?

The powerful and practical book will empower you to easily evangelize by inviting people into your life, your church, and into Christ. Feel the compassion of Christ. Participate in the harvest of souls for the Kingdom of God. Change your personal habits and church culture. You can share Jesus without killing relationships!

This book empowers all Christians everywhere to bring people to salvation! This is a simple yet profound book, carrying at its core, the mandate of the Christian Church in this age: GO and COMPEL.

In the book of Ezekiel, the prophet had a vision, where God shows him a valley full of bones. They were dry and brittle. I imagine sand blowing over the bones in desert heat. I imagine Ezekiel standing on a cliff that jetties out of the top of a sand dune as he peers over this valley. Then, God asks Ezekiel to speak to those bones. He asks him to speak---not just pray for the bones. So, Ezekiel speaks *to* the bones as God has given Him words to say. As he does...the bones begin to rattle and clink together. Can you imagine the sound of that? Bones were clinking together! Then muscles began to grow, then tendons, joints and then skin, eyes pop into sockets, hair grows back, and these once dry, brittle, and lifeless corpses become people resurrected to life again. (I would love to see this with the use of modern film-making). The dry and lifeless brittle bones were representing the people of God. Ezekiel, a prophet, was called out to speak a message to them.

While I am not claiming to be a prophet like Ezekiel, I have sensed the God of heaven's armies and my Best Friend speaking to me for some time to bring this message of *Invitality* to the church. Today, in obedience to the call of my Savior, in honor of His plan of redemption, and in expectation of a great swell of people being added to the church, I share this message. This is not because I am anything great in and of myself, but because I am a person God has chosen to bring a message and that message I must declare. This message is an encouragement, a comfort, a teaching, a paradigm shift, and a lifestyle change.

This message is a relevant call to an eternally relevant purpose.

This book is not meant to be read only. It is a tool that is meant to be applied in the spirit of Acts 1:1 "These things Jesus began both to do and teach."

For the reader's understanding of this book I will clarify how the book is organized.

- The beginning chapters address the heart.
- The middle chapters address the message.
- Later chapters address practical tactics.

1

Compelled

An aching began to birth in my heart years ago as I walked the campus of Iowa State University. Iowa State is a Land Grant University, which basically means for every building they put up, they have to leave a certain amount of beautiful green space. I know it took longer to get to class because I had to walk all of that green space, but it left me with a lot of time to think, pray, and enjoy God's beauty. As I walked the campus and prayed for my friends and for people with whom I attended class God began to break my heart for people. I began to realize that if God is going to reach people in the earth today, believers are going to have to step up and be the church we are meant to be. In order to reach people in real life, the life going on outside of the church walls on Sunday morning, we have got to get our tactics for reaching them out of the past and into the modern age. This means that we have got to get our thinking out of the past and into the modern age first.

When you declare that you are a Christian- that you believe in Jesus as the Son of God, that He died for your sins and was risen from the dead, and you make Him your Lord, the Bible says that you are saved from your sin (Romans 10:9-10). The Bible says that a place in heaven is being prepared for you. But the Bible also says that you join the Church. This is not a denomination. This is God's Church- His group of people called out of being bound by the sin of this world. You join The Church. The New Testament definition of the word *church* is literally a group of people "called out for a purpose." The church has been given a purpose from God- a mandate. The mandate is to evangelize the world. Let's define evangelism. Evangelism is the effective presentation of the gospel in a manner that the hearer understands its implications and is brought to a decision for Christ.

Now before you go and get scared about the word evangelism, I want you to take a deep breath. I want you to understand that evangelism is NOT always screaming at people on a street corner. It is not always standing on a stage in front of a huge group of people. Modern day evangelism is not about brow-beating someone into conforming to your expectations. It is about winning commitments to Christ. It is about a lifestyle of invitation. As Christians, we are to be people who invite others into our lives, into our churches, and into relationships with God through Jesus. That is what this book is all about.

In the Bible, the book of Luke, chapter 14, Jesus tells this parable. It is called the *Parable of the Great Supper*. A parable is a story with a meaning found in it. I ask that you read the following passage of scripture carefully with your heart open to what God may show you about its meaning. Here it is:

> Then He (Jesus) said to him, "A certain man gave a great supper and invited many, and sent his servant at supper time to say to those who were

invited, 'Come, for all things are now ready.' But they all with one *accord* began to make excuses. The first said to him, 'I have bought a piece of ground, and I must go and see it. I ask you to have me excused.' And another said, 'I have bought five yoke of oxen, and I am going to test them. I ask you to have me excused.' Still another said, 'I have married a wife, and therefore I cannot come.' So that servant came and reported these things to his master. Then the master of the house, being angry, said to his servant, 'Go out quickly into the streets and lanes of the city, and bring in here *the* poor and *the* maimed and *the* lame and *the* blind.' And the servant said, 'Master, it is done as you commanded, and still there is room.' **Then the master said to the servant, 'Go out into the highways and hedges, and compel *them* to come in, that my house may be filled.** For I say to you that none of those men who were invited shall taste my supper.'" (Luke 14:15-24)

Let me explain some of this parable to you so that you understand its significance. God, the Father is the "certain man" and Jesus is the "servant" sent to invite people for the "great supper" fellowship with the Father. The first group of people who he expected to receive His invitation (the Jewish people) came up with excuses. This is what any person does when their hearts are not softened to the Truth. So the "Master" Father sent his Servant Jesus to go after everyone else. He sent Him to anyone else who would receive His invitation to fellowship with Him. He said to Jesus Go and <u>compel</u> them to come in. The Master wants His House (the Church) full!

Now, without getting deep into theological discussion on end times events, nations of people, and things like that, I want you to especially focus on verse 23 above.

> Then the master said to the servant, 'Go out into the highways and hedges, and compel *them* to come in, that my house may be filled.' (Luke 14:23)

God wants His house, the church, full! And in order to get it full, he sent Jesus to the earth to die for humanity's sin and bring back fellowship. We just have to respond to the invitation. God the Father sent Jesus to complete a work of bringing humanity into fellowship with Him. Jesus started a work of invitation when He came to this earth. But Jesus is no longer on the earth physically. So, how is He going to do His Father's will and invite people to come into relationship with His Father? How will He continue to call people in the earth to come meet the Father God when He is in heaven? The answer is He is doing it today by raising up disciples to speak and minister in His place. He will finish the works He began in the earth through the church. If you believe in Jesus as your Lord, YOU ARE THE CHURCH. And God's will in the earth is going to get accomplished through you!

One can find this truth in Ephesians Chapter 1

> Now He (Jesus) is far above any ruler or authority or power or leader or anything else—not only in this world but also in the world to come. God has put all things under the authority of Christ and has made him head over all things for the benefit of the church. And the church is his body; it is made full and complete by Christ, who fills all things everywhere with himself. (Ephesians 1:21-23 NLT)

Do you understand what this verse is trying to say? Let's get some illumination on this scripture. The Apostle Paul is showing us that the Father God sent Jesus and made Him the Head of the church. Jesus is the head of the church and the rest of the believers in Jesus are His body. If the head has power above all the powers of darkness, so does the body! That should really make us think differently about what we are putting up with in our lives. Also, if the head decides that you are going to do something, the body listens and goes along.

Wouldn't it be an odd scenario just to disconnect your head and try to walk around? That is like the American saying "He is running around like a chicken with its head cut off." Farmers used to chop off the heads of chickens and the chickens would still run around the barnyard out of control with no sense of direction. The sad truth here is that some people do this in their relationship with God. They believe in Jesus, but when it comes to direction and vision, they detach themselves from the head- Christ. It's impossible to have direction without being connected to the head. Direction comes from the head. Understanding comes from the head. You may have a real strong body, but it is nothing without being connected to the vision that the head provides.

What does this have to do with evangelism? Jesus had a mission from His Father while He was on the earth. Go and compel people to come into the house of God. Compel people to come into relationship with the loving Creator. Compel them! Invite them! If Jesus had this purpose from God and He is the head, His body also has this purpose. Jesus' vision as the head is our mission as the body! He is charged to reconcile people to God and we are charged to reconcile people to God. Jesus, our head, has been given this great commission. We, the body, have been given this great commission also.

Here are some instances of Jesus communicating to us His great commission:

> Jesus came and told his disciples, "I have been given all authority in heaven and on earth. Therefore, <u>go and make disciples</u> of all the nations, baptizing them in the name of the Father and the Son and the Holy Spirit. Teach these new disciples to obey all the commands I have given you. And be sure of this: I am with you always, even to the end of the age." (Matt 28:18-20)

> And then he told them, "<u>Go into all the world and preach the Good News</u> to everyone. Anyone who believes and is baptized will be saved. But anyone who refuses to believe will be condemned." (Mark 16:15-18 NLT)

> And he said, "Yes, it was written long ago that the Messiah would suffer and die and rise from the dead on the third day. It was also written <u>that this message would be proclaimed</u> in the authority of his name to all the nations, beginning in Jerusalem: 'There is forgiveness of sins for all who repent.' You are witnesses of all these things." (Luke 24: 46-48 NLT)

> Again he said, "Peace be with you. As the Father has sent me, <u>so I am sending you.</u>" Then he breathed on them and said, "Receive the Holy Spirit." (John 20:21-22 NLT)

Now, let's go back to Luke 14 and really get an understanding of what this book is all about. Jesus is on a mission from God and we are too!

> Then the *Father* said to *Jesus*, 'Go out into the highways and hedges, and compel *them* to come in, that my house may be filled. (Luke 14:23)

Jesus' mission when He walked this earth was to be constantly compelling. He is still compelling today. Think about what He did while living physically on this earth. He shared from His heart. He prayed for people. He healed people. He did miracles. He took people with broken hearts and gave them fresh starts. He cried for and with people. He picked up children, hugged them, and blessed them. He traveled from town to town ministering to all sorts of people from all races, ethnicities, and backgrounds. He was dishonored by some, loved by others, and worshipped by others. <u>Jesus was compelling! His invitation to have a relationship with His Father was compelling! We are to be the same. We are to live a compelling lifestyle like His.</u>

Do you really understand what the word *compel* means? It means to urge, constrain, drag, herd, to bring about a course of action. (Merriam-Webster, 2013) Wow! When was the last time you looked at the people around you and thought, "What can I do to herd these people back into their rightful place of relationship with God?" When was the last time that you compelled someone to join in your life, your church, and most importantly your relationship with God? The truth is most people are more concerned with their day to day activities and the bills that are showing up in the mail than they are about other people's eternal destinies. We have to have a heart change.

"Do you not say, 'There are still four months and then comes the harvest? Behold, I say to you, lift up your eyes and look at the fields, for they are already white for harvest!" (John 4:35-38)

Today is the day. Now is the hour. There are people who are open to the good news of Jesus Christ living all around us. It is time for us to step over into the compassion of Jesus and look at people the way Jesus does. If we look at this world around us with our spiritual eyes, we will see people are hungry for the truth. People are starving and filling their spiritual voids by clamoring towards addiction, poor relationships, and the lust for power.

Don't just sit back, read this, and close off your mind to God's Word. Rather, I challenge you to open yourself up to His way of thinking and doing and live as a changed person to be more like Christ. It will be a great adventure. God is calling you to live beyond the status quo of what this world has to offer. He is calling you to be compelling. He is calling you to live out the great commission.

2

The Power of *Invitality*

Jesus started *Invitality* and we are to finish it! Invitality is a new word that I believe I received from God when studying along the lines of sharing the good news of Jesus with others. It means to live a lifestyle of compelling invitation. Some people are scared to the core when they think about standing on a street and preaching a message. Some people are scared when they think about getting in a debate with someone searching for Truth. But how about simply inviting a coworker into your life? How about inviting them over for a barbeque with your family and friends? How about inviting them to your church after that? As the relationship warms up how about inviting them to Christ? This is what *Invitality* is all about, a lifestyle of compelling invitation. As the church, we must come to the place where we say "God, I lay my life down on your altar. Lord, consume me with holy fire. Let me burn with passion for what you burn with passion for. Let me love people."

Here is an example of living with God's passion for people. Sheila had written off ever going to a church again after having a negative experience. She was a cutter. She had several tattoos and a lot of piercings. She was stared at years earlier in her only church experience and wasn't going to go through that again. She figured she would never be welcome at a church. But a person with *Invitality* built a relationship with her and she started to open up. One night in the work parking lot Sheila accepted Jesus. After about 5 invitations she came to church and felt the love in the church. Now she is trying to change jobs so that she can make church attendance a part of her life.

We have to come to a place as believers in Jesus that we choose to let others in on the goodness that we have enjoyed in knowing Him. Invitality is not a lifestyle of pushiness, but it is a lifestyle lived on purpose. It is purposely being unselfish with the goodness of God. God wants people to experience true salvation. True salvation only happens when there is faith in the heart of the person confessing Christ.

> For by grace you have been <u>saved through faith</u>, and that not of yourselves; *it is* the gift of God, not of works, lest anyone should boast. (Ephesians 2:8-9)

Faith is believing for one's self. When a person is pushed into a prayer, this is not salvation. This is mental assent to get you to leave them alone and move on. True heart faith will rise in people's hearts as we invite them into our lives, share with them the gospel, and invite them to receive salvation. I love how the New Living Translation puts this same verse:

> <u>God saved you by his grace when you believed.</u> And you can't take credit for this; it is a gift from God. Salvation is not a reward for the good things we have done, so none of us can boast about it.

Our lifestyle as believers in Jesus should be compelling to those that have no fellowship with the Father. We do have to give them space to come to a place where THEY BELIEVE. God is not into conformity from the outside-in. He is about transformation from the inside- out. He wants to make people completely new in Christ, not just a remodeled version of the old self.

> This means that anyone who belongs to Christ has become a new person. The old life is gone; a new life has begun! (2 Corinthians 5:17 NLT)

This is what Jesus was saying to the established religions of the day when He walked the earth. He wasn't concentrating on the rules and regulations, but on the hearts of people. Once God reaches the heart, He can bring new life. He can bring abundant life. He can bring fulfillment, joy, and purpose. We simply must choose to open up our lives and invite other people in.

I am reminded of one person that I had a chance to talk with recently. I first met Mick through a church member. He had no previous interaction with our church and it seemed like he wanted to remain that way. But how many people who don't know Jesus have a good impression of what a church is? Our first conversation was simply a "hi" and handshake. I smiled and listened on the inside just in case God wanted to show me something.

Through the course of day to day life, Mick and I had the opportunity for a second conversation. He ended up coming by my house and dropping his soon to be step-daughter off at our house to play with my daughter. We just talked on the front porch for a few minutes. There was nothing super deep about the conversation. We talked about his career as a plumber and I shared how God has blessed us with a house. We simply stood on the front porch for ten minutes "shooting the breeze." I think that God was just knitting a relationship, but for what purpose?

Our third conversation was when Mick and the church member wanted to talk to me about marriage. I told them what I tell a lot of people. "I don't do weddings; I do marriages---Christian marriages. A wedding is a one-time event. A Christian marriage is a life journey based on biblical standards." Since they came to me I sensed in my heart an opening to speak. I asked Mike if anyone had ever just simply explained the good news about Jesus to him. He said he went to church a couple times as a kid but never really caught the story. It is amazing how many people respond this way when asked. It seems America is full of mismatched and muddled head knowledge of Jesus from tradition, but lacking Word of God faith. I asked him if I could share it…and he said "yes." Notice that I asked. He gave me permission. In other words, His heart opened to what I had to say. I shared the simple gospel story and then invited him to pray and make Jesus the Lord of his life. Here is what I said. "So Mick… that is the basic story. Would you like to make Jesus the leader- the Lord- of your life today and receive salvation? "He simply said "yes…I would." We prayed together and a holy birth into the Kingdom of God took place. The angels rejoiced in heaven and I could sense his fiancé rejoicing on the inside as she sat in a chair next to us.

Have you ever had that happen? Have you ever been in a situation where you feel like you are exploding on the inside because you are so happy and excited, but, because of the moment, you can't let it out verbally? It feels like you are a pop bottle that has been shaken up and is about to be opened. I love this feeling! I get that feeling in my spirit every time I have the opportunity to share Christ and lead someone to experience their salvation.

Another man joined the Kingdom of God. How did it happen? *Invitality!* I simply invited Mick into my life, into the church, and to Christ. Glory!!! Today, he is still coming to church and is a proud father. I look forward to watching him grow into a spiritually mature believer.

Invitality is a compelling lifestyle of being open to other people around you. It is a lifestyle that decides that YOUR church isn't JUST for you. It is a lifestyle that decides that your whole life is an open book to be shared with others. Maybe that scares you a bit because you aren't perfect. You don't have it all together. Maybe a few un-choice words still flow out your mouth from time to time, maybe you have a temper, maybe you won't have every answer on every biblical subject known to man; I have something to tell you. Everyone already knows that! None of us are perfect. It is time that we get over our imperfections and fears and let God have His way in our lives.

There is a time for mass crusades. There is a time for getting blunt with sin. There is a time for in-depth conversation and <u>true</u> debate. However, in this day and age, in this modern society in which we live, I am convinced that most people will come to a true relationship with Jesus by someone inviting them into their life, into their church, and inviting them to know Christ. Massive crusades are still vital at times and the sharing of viewpoints is important, but in the end, it comes down to who Jesus is and what He offers.

Nobody truly likes a pushy salesman. In fact, if I am in a place where a salesman is being pushy, I simply leave. Seriously. I have just gotten to the point I don't put up with it. I just tell the guy or gal I am not going to put up with this and walk out. I don't do transactions this way. I know others wouldn't do this, but you would still shut down on the inside. I get up and walk out, but others walk out on the inside way before they walk out physically. I think this is determined by personality and how comfortable a person is with confrontation. No matter your personality, nobody likes a pushy salesman. However, if that salesman has something of value and he shares about it and offers me the chance to receive that item of value, I love to get it. This is the true heart of evangelism. The Bible says that it is the "goodness of God that leads people to repentance." (Romans 2:4)

Let me make this practical for you. We "need" car salesmen. We need this mediator-role to negotiate the deal. But no good car salesman ever goes to the customer and says "you are a true scumbag in your condition, and your car is a true piece of trash. How do you allow yourself to be so trashed? Take it from my experience, you need to receive this car and join my dealership and then you won't be looked at like a dirty, rotten, good for nothing auto driver with a rusty and junky car." That is like committing sales suicide. A good salesman highlights the goodness of what can be enjoyed, invites conversation around that subject, offers possibilities, and invites them to partake in an upgrade. A good car salesman helps people to realize their need and then helps them fill it. He doesn't bash them over the head with a picture of what situation they are in now. The people are driving the car every day and are fully aware of their condition. They drove, pushed, pulled, or dragged that car into the lot for goodness sake because they are tired of living in denial of their current condition. They are in the salesman's life because they want to know if there is something better. Let's keep it positive and invite them to enjoy what is available!

Invitality compels people with the goodness of God.

This lifestyle does not damn people for their current condition. It opens the door in safety. It is not pushy, but welcoming. Christ's Spirit is a spirit of hospitality. It has taken all the courage they could muster to put themselves around you in their current condition. They are thinking maybe there is something to this "God thing." Maybe there is even a possibility of having a real friend. They are still questioning if they want to open up to their current condition around you. Don't focus on their current condition. Invite them into your life through asking questions. Offer possibilities when the heart door is open. Then, when they have enough questions answered, invite them to partake in a life upgrade. They may have pushed, pulled, or dragged themselves in there, but they are going out riding in a new level of swag!

Sharing the message of the Kingdom of God is what God wants us to do and many people want to do God's will. However, the word "evangelism" is personally marred to many people. Maybe you can't think of this word without thinking of some visitor to your college campus standing on a box and yelling "you are going to hell." Maybe you can't think of the word without picturing a picketing sign, a person shouting "hater," or some other negative experience of the past. It is amazing how our experiences of the past try to shape our futures. I want you to take a moment and imagine all those negative paradigms that you have of evangelism from your past experiences. Now, imagine a big metal gray trash can. I want you to open up that trash can and throw all of those old ideas, experiences, and negativities away. Then, close the trash can. From this time forward, I want you to simply use this word "*Invitality.*"

I do not believe that evangelism is a bad word in and of itself. I believe evangelism is what this book is all about and I believe evangelism is needful in every generation of the body of Christ. Sharing the good news about Jesus with those around the world is a mandate of the church and I wholeheartedly share in this mandate. I just want you to get past any stereotypes that you have been holding onto or any stereotypes that have been holding onto you. If we are not careful, experiences of the past can stop us from moving forward with God. Stereotypes can shape our actions and words both good and bad. We often hear this only about the bad, but even good experiences of the past can box us in from moving forward with new methods of success if we are not careful. Some people get stuck in old ideologies. I don't want you to be stuck in the past. Evangelism can happen on a massive scale or a personal scale, but either one must have an element of invitation. Open your heart and mind up to God.

Yesterday's successful method of sharing Jesus could be less than successful in your situation today. A lot of people have been hurt by well-meaning Christians doing what they thought was effective in sharing the gospel. Maybe it was effective and acceptable in society twenty years ago, but is this the way society communicates today? Did you know that technology in some cases is doubling in its capabilities every ten months now? Things change. I know the gospel doesn't change, but the ways that people communicate effectively do. I don't believe pastors or believers purposefully try to offend people. I know that the message carries with it the ability to cut sharply. I know that not everyone is going to accept the Truth even if it presented 100% in love, but we need to do our part to be sharp communicators of the most important message ever.

I know there are people in churches all over the world who have brought friends to church only to have that friend become offended at the <u>way</u> the gospel message was presented. I am not talking about the message itself because I know that the Truth can cut deep and will cause a reaction. People were offended at Jesus and will be offended by the message from time to time. I am talking about the <u>way</u> the gospel message was presented. What happens next?

The church member gets offended at the church or the pastor and offense is never good! Offense opens the door to the enemy and all craziness can break loose. People react in different ways. Some people are verbal with their bad experiences and let everyone know it. Then others stuff resentment deep inside and simply stop inviting people. They are not going to risk a friendship on the <u>way</u> a message may be presented in a service. It's just how it is. Even if the message is this vital, people value their relationships. This scenario is not God's best!

It is time for us as the church to forgive one another for our faults and for experiences that have hurt us in the past. You may need to go to the person and talk through your experience and pray together. You may need to bless them with a copy of this book. God wants you inviting people into your life, inviting people into the church, and inviting people into Christ. You can't do that without a clear level of trust with your local church and a clean heart towards God. We are to love one another and then share that love with others. In most cases, it was not the message that was wrong. People seemed to be turned off by the tactic used to deliver the message. We will get into this in much more detail later in the book, but for now you must come to a place of giving your heart openly to a lifestyle of *Invitality*.

Jesus opened his life up to others and invited them to have a relationship with His Father. We need to do the same. We must live a lifestyle of compelling invitation. We must urge others with the heart of love into the Kingdom of God.

Pray, "Lord, please show me if I have taken offense or given offense in any way with the way your message has been delivered to those around me. Please forgive me and help me to forgive others. Today, I choose to let go of old paradigms and look to you for the best ways to reach the people around me with your Truth. Help me to embrace *Invitality*."

3

True Worship

Most times when you say the word *worship*, believers in Jesus think about songs and about music. They may also think about a type of service at church called a worship service. They may even think about a special event with a guest band.

But what does the Bible actually say about worship in regards to reaching people? Jesus says this;

> But the time is coming—indeed it's here now—when true worshipers will worship the Father in spirit and in truth. The Father is looking for those who will worship him that way. (John 4:23 NLT)

Did you notice it doesn't say true worshippers worship God "in music?" It doesn't say they worship God if they are on a church worship team or if they sing really loud at service each week. So really what this means is, if you want to worship God, you want to worship Him in reality all through your life. Everything you do in your life - your whole lifestyle is a lifestyle that places God as its first priority. Think of your whole lifestyle of *Invitality* as true and real worship unto God.

To worship the Lord, we must line up our words with our beliefs. Our conversations must have an eternal perspective. Our communication must always have a heart of evangelism to it. The way we talk and communicate with other people is worship unto God.

Sometimes people think you go to church and you worship at church, but really, actually, that's only a miniscule portion of what worship really is. Worship especially is outside the church building. We worship by what and how we do life. A big part of how we worship is in our conversations and in our attitudes. What do you talk about at work? What do you talk about on your phone with your family? What does your home atmosphere sound like to your kids? What attitude are you carrying around about your husband or wife?

I remember a season in my ministry where I worked as a children's pastor. It was amazing to hear what the kids would say. I love kids and have 5 of my own. They are filled with energy and often times speak the truth with no account for holding certain information back. Kids would come in to children's church and say things like "Mom said she didn't want to go to church today, but I made her come so I could learn more about Jesus." Or "Pastor Adam, I know I haven't been good today but can I PLEASE have some candy?" Or they would say things like "my dad called my mom this- *&^$#- and then they yelled at each other." I would ask if the child was ok and if the parents got it worked out and the child would say something like "I don't know, because it happened just now on the way to church."

Realize this: Words matter! Conversations matter! It's not just to the people directly involved in them, but also to those around us. They matter especially to God. We worship Him through our attitudes and actions- through our lifestyle every day. We should be giving God glory with our words. We ought to be sharing the goodness of Christ through the atmosphere of this world not the bitterness of the flesh.

Living a lifestyle of Invitality is living a lifestyle of true worship.

Let's look at this scripture again. Jesus says this:

> But the time is coming—indeed it's here now—when true worshipers will worship the Father in spirit and in truth. The Father is looking for those who will worship him that way. (John 4:23 NLT)

We are to worship God in spirit and truth. This means from our true selves- our spirit. You are a spirit being, you have a soul, and you live in a body. When the body dies, the eternal you continues living because you are an eternal being. You are a spirit-being made to worship God, spirit to Spirit. We will always be worshipping God, but in this earth we also worship God through the use of our body and through this mind which is being renewed as we learn. We worship God from our spirit ...and also in reality.

In other words, we worship God with our lifestyle outside of the church as much as we do when we hear music playing inside the church. Worship is not just a segment of a church service. Worship is not just done to music or with music. True worship is a lifestyle of honoring God through our attitudes and actions. You worship God with how you browse the internet. You worship God with your attitude toward your boss at work. You worship God through inviting other people to know Jesus. True worship unto God is NOT clubbing it up every day of the week and getting drunk with your homies and then coming into church one hour a week and acting like something you are not. That is not reality! Face the fact that you are a clubbing drunkard and get real with God about it. That is getting honest with God. He can work on that level of honesty if you are willing to come to Him. Better yet, decide to worship God out of the real you on the inside and not be led by your flesh or your desire to fit in with the social scene. You are a child of God created unto good works, not works that lead to death. Choose to let your spirit dictate your lifestyle. Decide to worship God with what you do with your body, mind, and spirit. Be real and honest, but be honestly godly!

True worship is becoming everything you are created to be 100% of the time. This means that we are called to live a lifestyle of worship outside of a church building. According to the New Testament, believers in Jesus are the church, not the building where they convene. This means that each day when you go to work, you take the church to the people. In doing so, you are really worshipping God by how you relate His goodness to others.

Let's be real. In general, people only remember ten percent of what you tell them, but they will remember about eighty-five percent of what they experience. When people experience you, they should be experiencing Christ's attitudes and actions. They should be experiencing God's love. Truth is- they should be so hungry for the goodness of God in you that they can't wait for you to invite them into your life. John Maxwell once said, "You teach what you know, but you reproduce who you are." If we are worshipping God in spirit and truth, we are connected with Him at all times. We are carriers of His presence to the workplace, the home, and yes, the church building.

I want to encourage you to BE a true worshipper of Jesus. Place your attitudes and actions in regards to sharing about Jesus at the foot of the cross. Place your lifestyle on the altar of worship unto God and let him mold and shape your life. Allow Jesus to revolutionize the way you think about evangelism. Most of all, allow Jesus to shape YOU. Let go of the old mindsets that have caused you to be lethargic in the sharing of God's goodness with others. Thoughts produce actions. If your actions are not bringing people to Christ, you must first let go of the thoughts that are stagnating you. Worship the Lord through sharing Christ. Do you realize that your very conversations in the workplace are a doorway for others to see and sense who God really is? Wow!!! That should put an end to workplace gossip and a beginning to workplace favor. Let go of lethargy and take on a new mindset of Invitality.

This means that your conversations wherever you go will testify to God's goodness and make a pathway for people to receive salvation. The word *testify* means

- To make a statement based on personal knowledge or belief
- Bear witness
- To serve as evidence or proof
- Express personal conviction
- Declare under oath
- Open declaration or profession, as of faith (Merriam-Webster, 2013)

We are the Church and we live in constant connection to the love of God. We live in constant connection to His goodness, His favor, His compassion, His forgiveness, His mercy, and His grace. It is easy to talk about, bear witness of, and express conviction about the Father when you are experiencing His greatness.

Let me tell you about something great I experienced. I had just come home from a long and busy morning. I walked in the door to my home and my wife put a pan of brownies in the oven. After about 25 minutes, the smell of those tasty brownies started to emanate through the atmosphere. Have you ever tasted warm brownies? That smell was almost unbearable in a good way.

Then, she pulled them out of the oven and she put marshmallows on top of them. The oven was still hot so she put the brownies back into it to melt the marshmallows on top. After a couple minutes, she pulled out the brownies again and put broken up graham crackers on them. Brownies hot out of the oven sure are a treat. We let them cool down just a little until we couldn't wait any longer. Then, we ate those brownies. They were like s'more brownies. Yum!

Are you hungry for them yet? Does that sound good to anybody? I would take one of those right now. Did you know that I don't have any problem telling you about those brownies? You don't have to force me to talk about my wife's brownies. They are good! Real good!

I just testified to you about my wife's brownies. This shows the power of experience, words, and atmosphere! The brownies are good, but God is better. I can testify just the same about something I experienced with God. You can too. Quit making it so difficult. If you can talk about brownies you can talk about your Savior.

I could have tried these brownies for the first time or I could have tried them 100 times and I would still testify about their goodness. It doesn't matter how long you have been a Christian. It doesn't matter how many experiences you have had with God. You could be a new believer or a veteran to the force. It doesn't take much to share a good experience. You don't have to force me to talk about those brownies. They were good. I just need an open door. You don't even have to ask me to tell the story. Just mention the word brownies and I feel an open door to share. I am not a brownie expert. I don't have a cooking PhD, but I do know I have experienced something great and I am not too selfish to share it with you. If we were together in person, I would offer you one right now.

That should be the way that we are in sharing our relationship with God. Has He given anybody peace on the inside of your heart? Has He given anybody joy? Has He given anybody joy in the midst of a situation that looked like total completely awful? Has He given you promises when you felt like you didn't deserve promises? Has He healed anyone's body? Has He done anything for your kids? How about your kids' kids? Yes, He has! So what are you waiting for? Share the goodness of those brownies!

I can just hear someone say. "It is more acceptable to talk about food than to talk about God." More acceptable to whom? Who are you living for? I live for an audience of one, my Savior. Who are you talking about? I am talking about what He has done for you. You are sharing your experience just like you share about your brownies. What is the big deal in that? This is worship as a lifestyle. This is part of Invitality. This makes you like a magnet to those who are searching for the Truth. Believe me, they are searching for Truth!

I don't have any problem testifying of God's goodness. I don't have any problem telling people I was healed of allergies. I never grew up with allergies, but in Iowa in the fall, there is something called ragweed. I suppose as the weather is drying out more and more in late summer, ragweed comes to full bloom. Anyway, one August/September my eyes started itching like crazy. I started sneezing all the time. I didn't know what was wrong. My eyes were all puffed up and I wore out my nose by blowing it on tissues repeatedly. I had never had allergies before. At the time, my eyes swelled up, itched, and it was unbearable. Those close to me said that it may be an allergy from something in the air during this season. I picked up some medication and "boom." It worked…mostly. My eyes were not itching and I could function but the medication made me dehydrated and sleepy. I knew this wasn't God's best but I made it through till the first hard frost when the ragweed went away. The next fall when the allergy came back, I decided that it wasn't God's best for me to live sneezing with my eyes puffy. I also decided I didn't want to live dehydrated and tired on medication. Medicine has its place, but I didn't want to live outside of God's best for me. I took authority in faith on the Word of God to receive divine healing and I was healed. I could go into detail on this and may in another book, but the point is simply that I am perfectly well without allergies and without any medication whatsoever simply by the healing power of God. He healed me! Did you read that? He healed me! I have been sick and I have been healthy. Being healthy is far better! God did it! I don't have any problem telling you about that. I experienced it and am thankful for it. I don't even need someone to push me to tell them the story. I just need an open door in conversation about sickness and there are plenty of those.

I don't have any problem sharing this with anyone. This is only one of many times God has healed me physically through His power. I love to testify of the things He has done for me. Do you see that this is true and real worship unto God? I am boasting on His goodness. He loved me enough to give me His healing power and can give that to anyone who will call upon His name. Who am I to hold back His goodness from others? That's how it is with our relationship with God in regards to our lifestyle of Invitality. We invite others into our lives as we testify of His goodness. This is how they get their first taste of the real God who is alive and impacting lives today!

Testifying is how we make them hungry for the things of God.

This is why God can say through the Psalmist "Oh, Taste and see that the Lord is good; blessed is the man who trusts in Him." (Psalms 34:8)

People want to have a taste. Our attitude of worship, wherever we are, gives them a taste of God. We can have this attitude at work and it is worship. People get a taste of God through your good attitude. Here is an instance that happened not too long ago.

There was a man named Denny who always came through the local business of one of our church members. After many days, what seemed like out of nowhere, this man walked across the business and said to the church member "listen, you are at work at 'sally-store,' what do you have to be so happy about?" The church member spoke to them about Jesus. After this Denny said, "Oh, you're one of them." But this isn't the end of the account. Shortly after the conversation, Dennis attended the church.

People get a taste through you inviting them into your life. Even our Godly attitude testifies of His goodness. You invite them into your life through sharing the goodness of God that you are experiencing. Do you want to live a lifestyle of true worship unto God? It will only happen if you make a purposeful and personal decision. It doesn't happen by accident. Life changes don't happen by accident. Sure, you change immediately in the short term the moment that you accept Christ as your Savior, but Lordship is an ongoing process. True success in life happens as we get the will of

God for our lives and then adopt His ways of being and doing. We are to be true worshippers.

We will see if you really make this decision based on the changes in your words and actions around others. If you say that you have made this change of heart and have become a true worshipper, then your life will change. If it doesn't, I doubt your decision. I know that is bold, but James 2:18 shows this to be true.

> But some will say, "You have faith, and I have works." Show me your faith without your works (this is impossible), and I will show you faith by my works. (James 2:18).

True heart faith is released through our actions. If you receive this message about true worship, then faith has birthed in your heart. Let it out through your lifestyle becoming one of Invitality. This will show you have accepted the message. Jesus thinks the same way about this. Jesus was very bold in Luke's account when he warned some people about hearing the message but not acting on it.

> "If you work the words into your life, you are like a smart carpenter who dug deep and laid the foundation of his house on bedrock. When the river burst its banks and crashed the house, nothing could shake it; it was built to last. But if you just use my words in Bible studies and don't work them into your life, you are like a dumb carpenter who built a house but skipped the foundation. When the swollen river came crashing in, it collapsed like a house of cards. It was a total loss." (Luke 6:48-49 MSG)

I know this is stern. But it's honest and real and that is where God's blessing resides. I love thinking of it this way. The book of John tells us that the harvest fields are ripe and ready to be harvested (the harvest fields are symbolic for people). Then it goes on to say that a harvester receives wages. That means there is a blessing reserved not just for the person receiving salvation but also for the person sharing it with others. Let's listen to the word that God is bringing and adjust our lifestyle so that we are reaching others, living on firm foundations, and walking in God's blessings!

Pray this with me now: "Father God, I open up my heart to your Truth. Your Word is Truth. I decide today to live a lifestyle of true worship before you. I realize that in order to do that, I must be a person who invites others to know you. I choose today to boast on the good things you are doing in my life for others to hear. I trust you to open doors for your glory in Jesus name. Amen."

4

Culture Shift

By all means, take what I am about to write personally! How did you get this book into your hands today? Most likely, you have heard about the book from someone else. It is possible that you saw it on the shelf and picked it up because of the "eye-candy" logo or design. But more than likely, you have decided to splurge on this spiritual book because of a personal recommendation.

Do you go to church? How did you hear about your church? Maybe you searched on-line or in the phone book at some point, but according to statistics most people go to a specific church because they were invited personally.

Recently, I completed a survey that I did in my own church. It is so important to know if what your church is doing to reach people is actually working. Otherwise, you may be failing miserably at reaching people, wasting tithes, and tacitly signing a church death certificate. In our case, as is the case of most churches around the body of Christ, most people came to our church because of a personal invitation. These were our top reasons people came to our church as guests in order of effectiveness:

- Personal invite   84%
- Church sign   8%
- The web-site   5%
- Other   3%

When I first received this information it blew my mind. I thought to myself that my responses must be off. I went back through the survey and recalculated to find the same results. After finding this out, I researched other church statistics and have learned that my findings are not unique.

According to a 2006 survey done by Lifeway Research, the research division of the Southern Baptist Convention, over 90% of new church members said they attended church for the first time because of a PERSONAL INVITATION. (lifewayresearch.com, 2006)

90%! These statistics are even bolder than mine! They are alarming! Think about what this could mean in reverse? If 90% who come do so because of an invitation and we are not out there inviting, what could be happening? This is dangerous information. This is powerful. I have to admit that I was a little skeptical when I first read this survey. I am an educated man and don't always take things just as people write or say them. In the Bible, the people in the church at Berea were the same way. In my desire to be thorough, I studied the details of this survey. I found out that they had surveyed 3000 people and that this survey followed scientific methods. This was a quality survey. Can you believe it? Up to 90% of people dawn the doorways of a church because they were invited. Can you see why this message of *Invitality* is so huge?!

Because of all this information I went to God in prayer about personal invitation rather than, first of all, how to make our church sign better or how to make our church website better. I believe the sign and the website are super important, but obviously the priority needed to be placed on personal invitation. We have 40,000 people drive by our sign a day, but personal invitation still works best! It's personal. The gospel is personal and people will come to know Jesus through relationships. According to statistics, even if you found the church on your own, the main reason you stayed or left that church was based more on your personal reception than even your convictions. It's all about personal relationships!

Sure, we would all like to believe that the reason we stay at a church or go to a church is based solely on the belief statement of that church. This just isn't true. A pastor could be the most awesome communicator in the world and have great doctrine, but if the people in the seats are mean and it's hard to build relationships, you are not going to stay long-term. There are people all over America and the world sitting in churches each week that don't believe everything that the church actually stands for. They are there because of personal relationships. Relationships are something that people intrinsically believe in. I am not going to offer you a long drawn out discourse on what I think of this. That's not the point of this book. In fact, if you are in a perfect church you are reading this in heaven. Churches are made up of imperfect people and there will not be a perfected church until Christ's return. You simply need to find the "perfect" church for you, and that church ought to have a revelation of the Great Commission.

The plan of God is personal. The Great Commission is personal. Invitality is personal.

One day a lady came into the break room at work and said "I'm new. What is the favorite thing that you like?" She was trying to get to know people, so she waited for the answer. "I am a Christian and I go to the best church in the world" is what the church member said. Then the church member just kept going back to it in conversation. Since this conversation, the new employee has been to the church four or five times and is getting closer to making a decision for Christ.

You have this book because someone recommended it. You are in a church probably because someone invited you. Statistics show us that at some point, some*one* invited you into their life, some*one* invited you into their church, and some*one* invited you into God's Church. Thank God for that person. Can you remember those people who helped you come close to God? Sometimes it is a parent, a mentor, or a friend. Other times, it is a coworker or a person that you happened to meet at the gym. This would be a good day to write them a personal thank-you note for living beyond their own egos. This would be a great day for telling that person that you will say a special thank-you to them by doing the same for someone else. The point is ITS PERSONAL! Occasionally, you will hear a spectacular story of a vision, a dream, or a near death experience someone had. But most often, the message of Jesus comes to you through a personal relationship. I love it!!! Let's not seek the spectacular and miss the supernatural. The way God works the majority of time is through people and through relationships. If you are going to be like Jesus, you are going to have to start liking people. His whole plan is personal.

Modern day evangelism is about adapting a New Testament lifestyle. That lifestyle is a culture of invitation. A culture is the set of shared attitudes, values, goals, and practices that characterize an institution or organization or social group. There are all sorts of social groups and each one of them is unique. (Beamer, 2011)

Cultures are powerful!

If you have had any involvement with drug culture, I can write these numbers 4:20 and you know exactly what I mean. April 20th and 4:20 in the afternoon is what drug culture says is "national smoke up day and time." This social group believes that a way they can bond is by nationally doing their illegal activity together at the same time. They have their own holiday that they share. It is based on the belief that marijuana should be ok for all to smoke and that they are going to "stick it to the man" to fight back. If you did not know this information, welcome to the 2000's. Personally, I love to watch who doesn't come into work for their shift on April 20th just for my own information. Their lifestyle is a culture.

If you have had any involvement with poverty culture, I can write this: *Section 8* and you know exactly what I mean. It means that someone else is going to pay some or all of your rent for you. Or it could mean that you only have to pay a portion of your rent for living in your housing. It means government aid. What *Section 8* actually refers to is Section 8 of the Housing Act of 1937, which basically grants rights to persons of low-income to have their rental payments made by the government of the United States of America. (Donovan, 2013) In some families living in poverty culture, meeting the requirements of getting onto section 8 means that they have reached independence.

I will never forget when a person who rented an apartment from me was rejoicing that her daughter was moving out and going to start her new independent life. I was glad for her. I love young adults and love to see them stepping out into new adventures. I simply said "Great, she must have gotten a job..." My renter said, "Oh no, she is pregnant and meets age requirements to get her own place on Section 8." She was good with that. Through conversation with the mother, I came to know that she had no other ambition for her daughter than she had for herself as a mom. Her family at this point shares poverty culture. Culture is super powerful. Any social worker can tell you that. Anyone who has fought their heart out to leave a poverty culture can tell you that. I am so proud of those who try to make a better life.

Whether you agree with it or not, you have to admit that there are a bunch of behaviors and belief characteristics that are shared within a social group. You may not have the slightest clue of where to go, what to fill out, which person to talk to, or what requirements are to take advantage of this program. This group of people knows their case worker's number by heart and have things figured out well in advance for their families, children, and friends. Their view of independence is shaped by their culture. Their view of life is shaped by their culture and their experience of life is shaped by their culture.

What do you think of when you say your church's name? What type of culture does your church have? Is your church the *friendly* church, the *middle-class* church, the *urban* church, the *spirit-filled* church, the *don't step on toes* church, the *young* church, the *"programs without relationships* church?" There could be all sorts of things that you think of. Whether you want to admit it or not every church has a culture. I want the culture my church to be one of *Invitality*. You may or may not want to admit your church culture. In order to find out what it is you will have to talk with all sorts of people within your congregation. It would be helpful to know it. Culture is made up of shared behaviors and belief characteristics. They are personal, but in a group they become congregational. Before you know it, they are systemic. If you can NOT say that the culture of your church is invitational, your church needs a culture shift. If you can NOT say that your personal life culture is invitational, you need a personal-life culture shift.

Truth does not change, but cultures shift. Sometimes they need to shift. Cultures shift and change to adapt and meet the needs and trends of current society. The Truth of the good news of Jesus Christ has not changed and will not change. Jesus will not change. His word will always stand the test of time and the changing of seasons. The Bible says ii Hebrews 13:8 that He (Jesus) is the same yesterday, today, and forever. Jesus and His Word don't change. They have no need to change. Jesus is the Truth!

Cultures and societies change, but Jesus has done all that is necessary for every person to be in relationship with the Father. He has already paid a ransom price for all humanity and risen from the dead. He is alive never to die again. The message is eternal, powerful, and miraculous. If we are to get this eternal message to the world, we must adapt our methods to be effective.

Imagine this- Yesterday, you were walking into the local grocery store and saw a group of people in bell-bottom jeans and flowered shirts. Some of the men had head bands in their hair. The girls had beautiful flowers in theirs. What is your first thought? You probably figure that they are going to a costume party of some sort.

Why is that? The movement characterized by that fashion has passed in its former state. What movement is that? It is the "Hippy

Movement" of the 1960's in America. So...you assume that they are going to some "spoof" event or party. Some may argue that the "hippy movement" is still alive and well. If it is, then they have changed the way they dress. Their "hippy culture" has changed a bit. They may still believe in making love and not war, but most hippies have had to get jobs and move on in their lives and adapt to the corporate culture of America in some way or another. Some are dealing with the raising of kids that happened through all of that "making love-not war" ideology.

What if these people you saw in the grocery store really were not going to a costume party? What if this is really how they dressed? What if these people were trying to sell you a really nice investment product? They would ask if you could sit and listen to them for a while. What if they would like you to invest your life savings with them? Would you have confidence in what they were trying to sell you? Most people would be concerned at some level. Their investment product could be the best product in the world, but the product is overshadowed by the ability of the people to be relevant with today's society. I don't mean they have to be exactly like you, but they are sporting outfits...and possibly ideologies from the 1960's. You would ask yourself questions like "are these people for real?" Can I trust the message here even though the messenger is so unique? You may even come to the point of believing in the product, but you just can't trust the person. What happens then? You walk away from this opportunity.

What I want you to see is that cultures are unique and they shift. The Truth of God's Word and the Truth of the salvation message will stand the test of time. It will never wear out. It is not a fad! The good news of salvation found in Jesus Christ is the best investment any person can ever make! The problem is the way you are communicating the gospel through your life may be looked at by others just like those people were looked at wearing bell-bottom jeans. Are you personally behind the curve and out of touch? Just because you have the best product known to man, does not mean that people will give you the time of day to share it with them. The message of Jesus dying on the cross for your sins and for your neighbor's sins will never fade away or change. It is of eternal value. The way that it is shared with those around us will need to adapt depending on culture. We, as believers in Jesus Christ, must always be on the look-out for effective ways to get the Truth to the people who are hurting.

Cultures vary by people group, location, language, and many other things. You can NOT assume you know your culture without stepping back to analyze it. Most people become somewhat blind to the culture that they live in because they grow used to it. Because culture is ever changing, it calls for the individual believer to be constantly changing. In the book of 2 Corinthians 3:18 it mentions that we are being changed from glory to glory. That means there is a former glory that is changing into a newer or better glory as we live in relationship with God. I believe that as we grow in our relationship with Christ, we should be getting better at sharing the gospel with effectiveness in our communities. We should get better and more effective at sharing His love with people around us. We should be going from a former state of glory to a better state of glory in our sanctification. Christ, through parables, miracles, healings…etc. was not only willing but able to adapt to the needs of culture. He adapted his tactic to the culture in order to be effective in His generation.

Let me ask you a question. Is your personal-life culture one that invites people to know Jesus? Maybe you thought that it was, but let's honestly look at your results. We can no longer sit back and point a finger at someone else and say "those people ought to do this and they would be better and sharing Jesus with others." Today, is the day for you and I to rise up, get up, and allow God to make something happen through our own life. Today is a day for us to stop looking outward and start changing inward. I say this because I am a believer. How long has it been since you shared the salvation message with someone? Think about it. What was the date? What was the circumstance? What did you say exactly? Are they sitting by you in church now? If you have trouble remembering the details of your encounter, it has been too long. If the Spirit of God is nudging you ever so gently right now, it has been too long. This should be on the forefront of our thoughts and lifestyle as a believer.

All culture change comes down to one person making a decision. That person is you!

It's time within the course of this book and your life to take a moment to stop worrying about "that guy" or "that girl." Stop worrying about this approach during a service or that style of music that is played. It is time to take a heart-look within you. You are the only one who stands in between a personal culture of invitation being effective for someone else's salvation. Stop thinking about the person who may say "glory, amen, or hallelujah" out loud at church if you bring a new person. Is God not bigger than someone's "amen?" Is God not bigger than a music set? Is God not bigger than your fear? I am not denying the reality of a good environment at all. I am trying to rid you of excuses. Didn't God reach out to you at some point?

> *Why limit His working in other people's lives because of your personal fears?*

If your church reaches you, why would you keep a good thing quiet? If the salvation of Jesus Christ has been good for you, it would be the most selfish thing in the world to shut your life off, shut your mouth down, and not share with those whom you say you love. What if someone would have been too scared to invite you into their life, into Christ, and into the church? I love this line from an album by Toby Mac. It says "open up your mind and let your soul be free. I can feel the Most-High shining on me. "C'mon, let's get this party started." (Mac, 2001)Let's go! Let's get this *Invitality* culture started in you! This is not just something that you do. This is who you are.

I love how Jesus answered the person who asked Him what the greatest commandment of all commandments was.

> Jesus replied, "The most important commandment is this: "Listen, O Israel! The Lord our God is the one and only Lord. And you must love the Lord with all your heart, all your soul, your entire mind, and all your strength.' The second is equally important: Love your neighbor as yourself.' No other commandment is greater than these." (Mark 12:29-31 NLT)

We are called by God to love Him and love others! If we love people, we will not hold back the answer to their pain, loneliness, or vanity. I know that I am suggesting a new way of life for many that are reading this. I know that means we have to think beyond ourselves and come to grips with the fact that we have had our focus inward rather than on others. This new way of life is actually a command from God.

> In Matthew 28 verse 18 Jesus is talking to his disciples after He had risen from the dead, and He says, "All authority has been given to Me in heaven and on earth. <u>Go therefore[c] and make disciples</u> of all the nations, baptizing them in the name of the Father and of the Son and of the Holy Spirit, 20 teaching them <u>to observe all things that I have commanded you</u>; and lo, I am with you always, *even* to the end of the age." Amen. (Mathew 28:18-20)

Christ has been given all authority and now He grants it to His disciples. When you become a believer in Jesus Christ and make Him the Lord of your life you are enrolled as a disciple. The word disciple means learner or trainee. We, as believers, are commissioned by Jesus to be learners and to help others learn about the Kingdom of God. You have been enrolled in discipleship school. That discipleship school, or relationship with God, has one intense purpose associated with it: Go!

Go, and share the goodness of what it is like to be in a right relationship with your Creator. Help others experience what you have. Go!

This is actually a command. It is not a suggestion. Christ did not say to go only when you feel like it, only when the government says it's ok, if you are a Sagittarius, if you have blonde hair, or if you are in shape. No! This is a command. Go! I don't know about you, but by personality I hate being commanded to do something. My first reaction to an order is always to try to buck the system. Having children has taught me a lot about God and about life. I guess I have the personality trait of a two-year-old sometimes with God. That is humbling.

If you tell a two-year-old to go get their pajamas on, they will yell back at you "no." When this first happens to a parent, it is a life transforming moment. It is where the rubber meets the road. It is where we decide who is in charge in the house and who is not in charge. God designed kids to be like this. It is not a bad thing if it is met with good parenting and good boundaries. This "power struggle" is actually good for the child because the child learns where boundaries are and how to function in his/her role in the home. Later, this helps them submit to God's call and still have the backbone to accomplish it. They are learning the culture and where they fit. I am helping you to realize your culture as a Christian and where you fit.

This experience with my child helped me to accept this command from God. He says to "go" and like a child or like Jonah in scripture, we may want to say "no." God tells us to go make disciples because He has our best interest in mind. He knows that in the process of going and making other disciples, we will find fulfillment in this life and help others to find it also. I don't tell my two-year-old to put on pajamas simply because I get some special kick out of it. I tell him to put on pajamas so he is not cold overnight. You can't always reason with a two-year-old. They don't always get "higher reasoning." You can't always reason with an adult. But you can help them to understand a command and do it, trusting that they will understand later, and experience what's best for them in the big picture scope of life. It's God's higher reasoning. This is what God has done by commanding us to "Go." We may not understand all of the reasons why, but when we submit to God, our life journey is much better. Remember what God said through the prophet Isaiah;

> "For My thoughts are not your thoughts, nor are My ways your ways," For as the heavens are higher than the earth, so are My ways higher than your ways, and My thoughts higher than your thoughts" says the Lord. (Isaiah 55:8-9)

It is in our best interest to heed God's command and share the good news of the Kingdom of God. If we do not share the good things we experience in Christ, we become like a dead sea. A body of water is meant to have water flowing in and water flowing out. The blessing of salvation and all the other things that God brings to us through Christ represent rivers of life-giving water flowing into us. However, do you have any sort of outlet for those rivers of blessing?

> He who believes in Me, as the Scripture has said, out of his heart will flow rivers of living water."
> (John 7:38)

Have you ever seen a pond without any outlet? A pond without any water movement in it grows scum! That is my "technical" word for the green mass of nastiness that covers the top of a motionless body of water. It makes it so that it stinks. It makes it no good for fishing and I like fishing. It makes it no good for any animal life. I do not believe that pond scum is God's will. A body of water is meant to have water flowing in and water flowing out. It is meant to sustain and give life. This water flowing in and out helps to give proper and healthy balance as God intended. It's better for the pond's health and the entire habitat around the pond. The same is true of the believer. We are meant to experience God's goodness and to let that flow out to others. We are created to live in a habitat of Invitality. It's in our best interest to go and share with others because then we don't grow spiritual pond scum in our lives. Of course it is in others best interest that we live this lifestyle or they would not hear the message of salvation.

Have you ever seen a pond that started out healthy but through drought or something else has grown stagnant over years? This is what can happen to someone who once was excited to share his/her faith. You may have started with some fire, but that does not guarantee you have fire to share today. If we are not purposeful, the cares of this life will come in and dam up the area of outflow in our life. Then, a person begins to grow scum. Before you know it, you are sharing your scum around the earth and wondering why people who know you and are around you are not accepting this same Jesus that you have accepted.

You may not realize you are scummy but may say things like "where is the life that I once felt in following Christ?" or "I'm not feeling the same vibe I used to feel." This is what happens when the life is starting to leave the pond, but the full scum has not started to show up. Quick! Make a heart change. If you don't make a heart change, soon you will start to focus on and say these things- "it's just not the right music to reach people here" or "our church is too hot or too cold in the sanctuary" or "if we had a different pastor we would grow this church." This is where offense creeps in. If you do not check your attitude toward God at this crucial point you are leaving yourself like a pond unattended. This is where years of little things become big issues in your life and you lose focus on the big picture of reaching people for Christ. Focus becomes inward only and damaging to self and others. You have become a scummy pond and need a refreshing blast of God's Spirit, forgiveness, and a fresh start in going out in the Great Commission again. I sense that there are going to be thousands that read this and say "oh God, that's me." Well, what are you waiting for? Repent.

It only takes a moment to repent to God. Ask forgiveness and confess your sin. Go to your pastor and ask forgiveness. Share with those closest to you in life what God has shown you. They have been experiencing your pond scum stench and putting up with it. Ask forgiveness as necessary and let's get going! Life is too short to wallow in the past. Once it is dealt with, let's move on.

If you want to clear up that pond of your life, give it an outlet. Give it somewhere to get out. Give it some water flowing in and water flowing out. All of a sudden, supernaturally, what will happen is all that green muck and algae, all that scum growing on the top dissipates. Life starts to be reborn. The fish start showing up again. Stuff can live around you. You will find yourself to be happy! You actually become happy because life isn't just about you anymore.

Read this out loud and declare it from your heart. Make a personal commitment with God today!

Today, I declare a new personal culture for myself. From this day forward, I will learn and live a lifestyle of invitation. I will have an open heart, an open life, and open doors to all people. I will openly share the good news about salvation found in Jesus Christ. I choose to be flexible in my service, full of grace in my judgments, welcoming to the lost, and celebrating with those who are found. The Holy Spirit is my witness this day.

Signed_____   Date _____

5

Powerful Prayer for People

Simply put, prayer is communication with God. The point of prayer is to have fellowship with the Father, His Son Jesus, and the Holy Spirit. When we pray, we get God's perspective on this life and on His plan for the earth. When we communicate with God we catch His heart and His passion. His heart and His passion is people. He created all people for fellowship, but many people are not able to enjoy His company. He pursues those people through empowering believers and sending us out to share His goodness with others.

There is much to be said of prayer, but the sake of this book we will focus strictly on prayer for those who are separated from God by their state of unbelief. They abide in a sinful nature far from God. Oh God, help us to catch your heart for these people. One chapter is not enough to exhaust praying for the lost, but this will be a great start for all people serious about embracing *Invitality*.

Prayer is not meant to be something that comes with flowery words of man's wisdom. Prayer is real heart to heart conversation with the Father. Prayer is not supposed to be hard to understand or hard to do and it's not. I love to sit down with a cup of coffee and just talk to God and listen to what He has to say in my heart. Sometime on vacation I will slip down to the dock at the lake and throw in my fishing lure and just ask God if there is anything He wants to tell me. Pretty much daily, I ask the Lord, "How are you doing today?"

Worship is the real you. Prayer is the real you having a conversation with God. Conversation is a dialogue, not a monologue. That means it's a 2-way street. We talk and then we listen. We listen because He wants to share with us what to do with our lives. We listen because He wants to have us declare things into the earth through our words.

John Wesley said "God does nothing except in response to believing prayer" (Wesley, 2013). Your life to this point is a result of your choices, your words, and your prayers. When we pray, we are allowing God's will that is done in heaven to be birthed into this earth. We are enabling God's will to be done in the earth.

Remember in Luke 11:2-4 we see a model of how we should pray. It is a model, an outline, a cut-out, and a structural example of how a person can pray. It does not mean these are the only words you can say.

> So He said to them, "When you pray, say:
> Our Father in heaven,
> Hallowed be Your name.
> Your kingdom come.
> Your will be done
> On earth as *it is* in heaven.
> Give us day by day our daily bread.
> And forgive us our sins,

For we also forgive everyone who is indebted to us.
And do not lead us into temptation,
But deliver us from the evil one." (Luke 11:2-4)

I want you to focus on these "Your KINGDOM COME, YOUR WILL BE DONE ON EARTH AS IT IS IN HEAVEN" Please understand that God is not in control of every detail that goes on in the earth. God is not causing murder. God is not killing babies. God is not even making you sick. These are the results of sin in the earth. God has an answer for these issues. I could go real deep in teaching here but I must stay on topic. God wants to bring His love, compassion, blessing, and forgiveness to the earth. He wants all to experience His salvation!

Then why doesn't He just set up a loudspeaker from the heavens and declare salvation and save everyone? Simply put, in the book of Genesis, Adam sinned and gave legal dominion of this earth over to Satan. Satan has dominion here over all things not of God. This is his kingdom for now. We are here, but we are born again through salvation in Jesus Christ. Now, we are of the original godly kingdom. We are of the kingdom of light. We are of the kingdom of God's dear son. This is why the Apostle Paul wrote that we are in the world, but not of it.

Now, Jesus came to earth and paid the debt that needed to be paid for all humanity to be set free from the legal dominion of Satan. People have been set free. However, this earth is still under Satan's dominion until his lease expires. One day Jesus will come again, the lease will be totally expired, and that nasty devil will be done away with for good!

For now, God gets his will done in the earth primarily through His people. They fellowship with God and He shows them what His will is in a given situation. Then the believer asks for those things to be done and declares, or speaks, or acts those things into existence in this realm. Often times, people don't realize they are declaring His will into their lives in this realm but they are. For example, when you pray, if you take the time to say thank you to God for answering your prayer in a given situation, you have declared it into this earth. You may not have realized you were confessing it into this earth, but the spiritual principle is there and working whether you knew it or not. Once you know how this works, you can do it on purpose and you will see more answers to your prayers.

When we, as people located on the earth, ask God for things, it gives God legal right to birth them into this earth. We have no rights in and of ourselves, so God grants us the use of the name of Jesus. Jesus has the rights because He paid the price to get them back from the enemy and then rose from the dead. We use the name of Jesus as our spiritual legal tender to appropriate God's will into our lives and into the earth. Praise God, there is no distance in the spirit realm and we can affect change all over the world right from our living room in prayer.

This is pretty in depth, but it comes down to this. We are to pray to the Father God, in Jesus name, thank Him for what we have received, and we will see it in our lives.

It's that easy. Now let's get back to reaching people for Jesus with our prayers. We see in God's word that he wishes all people to be saved and come to the knowledge of Jesus. We know that this is God's will. His word is His will. We don't need an eight-hour special prayer service to know this. He wrote us a tangible letter that we can read and made it easy. Since we know it is His will and it is what He wants done in the earth, we need to ask for it and get it done for Him in the earth.

> Therefore, I exhort first of all the supplications, prayers, intercessions, and giving of thanks be made for all men, (for God) desires all men to be saved and to come to the knowledge of the truth.
> (I Timothy 2:1, 4)

God wants people to receive salvation in the earth, but he is not here. He must get it to the people through believers (Kingdom of God Ambassadors) in the earth. He wants people so bad that he sent His only Son to die for them and pay the price. He actually asked His Son, who is God, to put on mortality and go through this life, so that we would have the capability of getting our prayers answered. Let's step up and pray!

What do we pray for? Pray for the people in your sphere of influence by name. Stop right now and make a list of people in your daily sphere of influence who you think might now know Jesus. If there is a questionable person, write the name down. We don't want anyone to miss out. Now God will have you pray for nations and He will have you pray for cities and things like that, but we are focusing on *Invitality* here. We are focusing on the primary place that God has called you to reach. We should not spend all of our time in prayer for another nation and ignore our primary mission field right where we live. Let's look at how Jesus told us to pray for our mission field.

> Then He said unto them, "The harvest truly is plentiful, but the laborers are few; therefore, pray the Lord of the harvest to send our laborers into His harvest." (Luke 10:2)

This is very interesting because Jesus said this to people whom He had already trained up to be laborers. They were Kingdom

Reps and they were soul winners. He wanted his believers who were sent out to preach to also pray that more people would be sent out to preach. We are also Jesus' disciples in the earth today. We are sent to preach the gospel message. Yet we are commissioned here to pray the same way that these disciples were. We are to pray and ask the Father to send out laborers.

Wait a minute. Can't God just send who He wants to send? Why do we have to ask? Isn't He God and can't He do what He wants? If this were the case, then there would be no pain in the earth and there would be no death. Then people would stop asking the question "If God is real, why is there all this pain in the world?"

He is God, but He bound Himself, because of His choice to give humanity free will way back in the Garden of Eden. Do you see what I am saying? His will is to have plenty of laborers preaching the good news in the earth, but He can't take authority that He doesn't have. He has to flow within the laws that He has established. These are kingdom laws. Like I wrote before, the way He gets His will and His messengers into the earth is by us asking for them and declaring it done. He is God and He makes the laws, but He cannot break them whenever He wants to. His word is His bond. His word is never changing. The enemy may have a lease that is running out, but God has a way to reach the people that are still under the bondages of that lease. The way is by sending out laborers with the message of freedom from the kingdom of darkness.

Laborers are called by God, trained,
and sent out as people pray.

We are to ask God for more laborers. We don't have to ask in a special "New King James Version" of speaking. We just ask God from our hearts- man to God. Then say "thank-you" for what we asked for. God is so good and desires so much that someone would pray and give Him license to send more laborers. You are welcome to pray this more than once. Sometimes we have a good meal and think we will never eat again only to realize a few hours later that we are hungry. There is still a need for food. There will always be fresh need for people to be saved as long as babies are being born. So, please pray.

You don't get an answer to your conversation with God because you ask a certain number of times. So don't think that you will sit down and pray the same words fifty times and then God will be like "OK, you have earned my answer." We don't earn laborers by our length of prayer or number of times we pray something. The Father's heart is to send laborers. We just need to release His heart. He responds to our faith. That is our simple belief that He will give us what we are asking. And He will send laborers because He wants to.

I don't give my kids food for dinner because they ask me fifty times. I give them food for dinner because they come to me and say "Dad, I am hungry. Will you please get us some dinner?" That doesn't change my heart, because I always want all my kids fed and healthy. That gives me the ability to meet the need that has been recognized. In this case, I call the pizza place that is on speed dial and take care of the need. Rest assured that it is possible and plausible that they will come back again and ask for food. I am not upset. There is a fresh need. Let me take care of that need. This is how God is with us. He knows there is a need for salvation always coming up in the earth and wants to meet that need. When we ask

Him, He says "Sure and thanks for coming to Me and letting Me get involved to meet the need."

We are to pray for laborers to be sent and we are to pray that doors would be opened for the laborers to walk through. The concept of doors is very interesting in scripture. As you study the Bible, you see that there are tangible or "concrete" doors mentioned in stories. There are figurative doors mentioned in parables and about people's hearts and minds. Then there are real and spiritual doors that cannot be seen physically. These spiritual doors are gateways that bring supernatural things into the realm that we see with our naked eye. The spirit realm is real and we must take our authority in Christ there before it ever shows up in our physical vision and in our physical life. This is what Paul says in Ephesians 6 that we wrestle not against flesh and blood (people), but against principalities, powers, and rulers of darkness of this age, against spiritual hosts of wickedness in the heavenly places. The real battle is in the spirit realm. This realm is just an outworking of what is going on behind the scenes.

We are to pray for spiritual doors to open. When the spiritual doors open, people's hearts, minds, and schedules (figurative doors) become open to the sharing of the gospel. Witnessing for Christ without praying for open doors is trying to bring the power of God in your own strength. It works by His grace through faith, so don't waste your time. Pray for doors to be opened! Paul tells us to do it. This brings success and makes things much smoother when we are out there inviting people into our lives.

> Continue earnestly in prayer, being vigilant in it with thanksgiving; meanwhile praying also for <u>us that God would open to us a door</u> for the word to speak the mystery of Christ, for which I am an

> ambassador in chains, that I will make it manifest as I ought to speak. (Colossians 4:2-4)

Notice that Paul is asking for prayer from other people so that doors would open to proclaim the gospel. He can't open every door on his own. We can't open every door on our own. We need people to pray and ask God to open the doors. Can't God open any door? Remember, He has the ability and strength to do it, but He does not have a license to do it until we ask Him to do it. Now, look at the scripture again and notice that Paul writes to pray with thanksgiving. Why? Because this thanksgiving is the declaration of God's will being done. When we declare something done as God's ambassadors, it gives Him license to change things and birth things into this earth. If we pray and ask that spiritual doors would be open, we can trust God to have it done when we go to reach our sphere of influence. Let's pray.

Paul, in the letter to the Corinthian church, is writing about spending time in the city of Ephesus. It is interesting what he writes.

"For a great and effective door has opened unto me and there are many adversaries." (I Corinthians 16:9)

I believe that Paul is acknowledging a figurative and spiritual door. I believe also that the adversaries he was facing were spiritual first. Then, the spiritual forces were working on the hearts of non-Christian men. This sounds just like trying to reach people all over the world today. We need people to pray. Before you go out to reach your sphere of influence, pray that a door would be opened unto you. Call a friend whom you trust and love and have them pray with you and for you also that a door may be opened. Be earnest about it. Persevere in prayer and don't give up or give in.

> *Pray for laborers, pray for open doors to speak, and pray for effectiveness!*

> Continue earnestly in prayer, being vigilant in it with thanksgiving; meanwhile praying also for us that God would open to us a door for the word to speak the mystery of Christ, for which I am an ambassador in chains, <u>that I will make it manifest as I ought to speak.</u> (Colossians 4:2-4)

So many people want to do right. They want to share the gospel with people, but they try to do it without prayer. Prayer sets down the railroad tracks for the train of the gospel to come in on. Prayer unleashes the Holy Spirit presence of God to work behind the scenes on your behalf. I believe in education. I have two bachelor degrees. I am working on my second master's degree. One of my bachelor's degrees is in Speech Communication, but I don't dare to try to share with someone out of my formalized book training alone. Sure God can use my formal training and does use it, but the goal of Invitality is the effective presentation of the gospel in a manner that the hearer understands its implications and is brought to a decision for Christ.

We deliver a message, but the Holy Spirit does the convicting. I could speak until I am blue in the face using the wrong approach and have zero results. I can ask one question anointed by the Spirit of God and the person could be putty in God's hands. We want effective speaking. We want effective manifestation of gospel power. We want it to come out in the <u>way</u> that God needs it to come across to the other person.

I am reminded of what brought a girl named Jackie to church. She works in a deli. She didn't feel comfortable coming to the church because if issues and insecurities, but a person with Invitality just stayed in her life sharing the goodness of God. Then one day this person looked at Jackie and said, "Look, if you don't want to have fun- don't come. But if you want to have fun, I challenge you to come and sit more than one time." After three times sitting in church she gave her heart to Christ. God will give you the words to say and the right <u>way</u> to say them.

---

*A word fitly spoken is like apples of gold
in setting of silver. (Proverbs 25:11)*

We must do our part to prepare both naturally and spiritually to reach our sphere of influence. We bring the natural and the supernatural together to make an explosive force for God. Think ahead and prepare a plan, but pray ahead and get the Holy Spirit's direction. We must understand that we are the sowers of the Word of God. In Christ's parable of the sower, only twenty-five percent of people showed lasting fruit from the message of Christ. Of those who showed lasting fruit, some produced thirty-fold, some sixty-fold, and some one-hundred-fold. Jesus is trying to show us that we are called to go out and reach people and that we are in a supernatural work, but there will be varying results. We can do our part spiritually and naturally to prepare the way ahead of time to have the best results available. In understanding God's word, we can have realistic expectations and do our part to achieve success. We prepare people to receive the message by praying for the laborers to communicate effectively.

We must also understand that we are not the only ones praying. There are people all over the world praying. We enter into their prayer labors to reap the harvest when we obey the Great Commission to go.

> And he who reaps receives wages, and gathers fruit for eternal life, that both he who sows and he who reaps may rejoice together. For in this the saying is true: One sows and another reaps. I sent you to reap that for which you have not labored; others have labored, and you have entered into their labors. (John 4:36-38)

When you pray, ask your Father in your own words for more people to be sent out, ask your Father to open doors for you and others to speak, and ask God to make you effective in both giving out the message and in their reception of it. Ask for people to receive the message of the Kingdom of God.

6

Preach what Jesus Preached

How then shall they call on Him in whom they have not believed? And how shall they believe in Him of whom they have not heard? And how shall they hear without a preacher? And how shall they preach unless they are sent? As it is written:

> "How beautiful are the feet of those who preach the gospel of peace, who bring glad tidings of good things!" (Romans 10:14-15)

As a believer in Jesus Christ, you are called to preach.

People can't call on whom they don't believe. People can't believe without hearing the gospel. People can't hear without a preacher. We are called to preach. I can hear you saying "I'm no preacher." You are a preacher. You may not be a pastor, prophet, evangelist, teacher, or apostle, but you are a preacher. Every believer has been given a mandate from God to "go into all the world and preach the gospel. (Mark 16:15-18).

Now, the evangelist has a calling and separation from God to equip and edify the body of Christ to reach people. They are to train the body of Christ to be effective at reaching people. They also tend to reach masses of people with their ministry from God. Most people are not evangelists, but all believers are still called to preach the gospel and bring people to Jesus. It's kind of like this example- You may not be a chef, but you still cook for your family. The chef cooks on a different scale. The chef's called to feed the masses and to train people how to cook. You are called to feed your family and your sphere of influence. You are called to preach in your area of influence.

> For since, in the wisdom of God, the world through wisdom did not know God, it pleased God through the foolishness of <u>the message preached</u> to save those who believe. (I Corinthians 1:21)

The word *preach* means to declare, it means to declare an event; to proclaim; to herald (Vines, 2013). It is like declaring something to a group of people on a verbal billboard. Our responsibility and honor as Christians is to preach the gospel. We preach the message and He does the saving. Teaching is to explain the Bible and all these things. We are not all called or gifted to teach. We are all called to preach. Your proclaiming the gospel message will sound different from someone else's but the message should be the same. Our message should be the same message as Jesus: The Kingdom of God. The Kingdom of God has arrived.

Saint Francis of Assisi once said "preach the gospel at all times and when necessary use words." (Assisi, 2013)

I am here to tell you that it is necessary to use words! The Bible says that it is by preaching the gospel that people are saved. It is by hearing and understanding the message that they receive faith to be saved by God's grace. Preaching is necessary. I have seen people use this statement as an excuse to wear a Christian T-shirt, put a fish on their car, or give in an offering, but never tell people about Jesus. Proclaiming the good news that the Kingdom of God is here is necessary!

You may choose to proclaim it on a billboard. You may choose to proclaim it through video. You may choose to proclaim it through art. Whatever you do, do NOT stop declaring it with your mouth. When you declare the gospel it births power into this realm for people to receive salvation from God and to enjoy all His power.

> For I am not ashamed of <u>the gospel</u> of Christ, for it is the power of God to salvation for everyone who believes, for the Jew first and also for the Greek. (Romans 1:16)

I once heard an atheist orator say that he didn't respect anyone who claimed to be Christian and yet didn't tell other people about it. He said that if you really believe there is a hell and heaven and don't tell others about it, then that is like seeing someone about to be run over by a diesel truck and doing nothing about it. When I heard him say this I had to agree. This is why we need preaching. This is why we need proclaiming. We believe in the truth and must walk in love and share it with others.

As you see a diesel truck coming down the road about to hit someone, you may say "hey...hey you...get outta the way." The closer the truck came to the person, the more desperate you would become. Until at the last moment, you would yell out "Get out of the way! Save yourself!" You would move into action and dive out there at the risk of your own life and tackle them to safety.

You would not stand on the side of the road and try to teach them how trucks work and how their body will be smashed. That is not the time for teaching. There is a time for it for sure, but this is a time for proclaiming. I am here to tell you today by the unction of God that we are in a day where the Kingdom of God is here and that the kingdom of darkness is real. The end of all things is around the corner! Now go and declare it and save people from the kingdom of darkness!

> And this gospel of the kingdom will be preached in all the world as a witness to all the nations, and then the end shall come. (Matthew 24:14)

You can proclaim all sorts of things, but that doesn't mean that you will have Jesus' results in your life. There is only one way to get the same results He did and that is to preach the same thing he did. Jesus taught and preached the gospel of the kingdom of God. Because this book is on Invitality, we are focusing on the preaching part.

> And Jesus went about all Galilee, teaching in their synagogues, <u>preaching the gospel of the kingdom</u>, and healing all kinds of sickness and all kinds of disease among the people. (Matthew 4:23)

People get upset because they don't see salvations, they don't see healings, or they don't see people getting needs met, but the power is on the gospel message. The gospel is the power of God unto salvation. The gospel makes way for the power to show up. What Gospel is that? It is the gospel of the Kingdom of God. If you preach a theory, if you preach an experience, even if you preach that Jesus is your best friend, but you don't preach the gospel of the Kingdom of God, you won't have the same fruit. Preach what Jesus preached. Share what Jesus shared and you will have the same results.

What is the gospel of the kingdom of God exactly? The word *gospel* simply means good news (Vines, 2013). It is great to have some good news. What is the good news of the Kingdom of God?

The gospel of the kingdom of God is the good news about God's kingdom. The word *kingdom* comes from two words: 1) King and 2) Dominion. So, we are simply talking about the King of the kingdom of God and His dominion (Vines, 2013). The King of the Kingdom of God came to earth. His name is Jesus. Jesus has paid the ransom price to save all people who are under the dominion of the kingdom of sin. All humanity, because of Adam's sin in the Garden of Eden, is under the dominion of sin and must be freed from this dominion. The price that has to be paid to free someone from this kingdom of sin is death. Jesus paid the ransom price through His death on a cross for all humanity's sin for all time, buying the human race back out of slavery in the kingdom of sin. After being dead three days, Jesus rose alive from the dead. He showed Himself alive to many people before ascending into heaven to take His position at God the Father's right hand. He is alive today reigning over His kingdom from heaven. He then delivered His authority to His people in the earth that believe on Him. His people can walk in His authority in the earth today just like He did when He was on the earth. Jesus told us the Kingdom of God is here. The kingdom of God is a spiritual kingdom that is present with God's people today.

Because of what Jesus did, the rule of God has altered the limits sin has previously placed on individuals (Hayford, 2002). No longer do we have to be subject to our flesh or to our old ways of thinking. The devil and all his wiles no longer can keep believers bound. The believer lives as a ruler on Christ's behalf in the world. We no longer have to be subject to this world's order. The believer in Jesus is in this world, but not of this world's system.

Accepting the true account of Jesus' vicarious life, death, and resurrection as a ransom price for you and confessing Jesus as your Lord takes you from being subject to the kingdom of darkness and places you into the kingdom of God. Spiritually, you move kingdoms. You are made new. Your potentialities change! You are now an ambassador of the realm, reign, and regency of God Himself. Accepting salvation begins the reinstatement of your dominion under God through the power of the Holy Spirit. His Holy Spirit now lives in you, equips you, guides you, and can empower you for everything you need for life on this earth and beyond. When we believe in Jesus we become God's administrators in the earth. This shows up in our lives as righteousness, peace, and joy in the Holy Spirit.

I know this is a lot to take in if this is your first time reading this. You may want to go back and read this section again. Maybe you have heard this message through other lingo before, but rest assured this is what Jesus was teaching and preaching. Rest assured that this is what the apostles were teaching after He went to heaven. This is taught and lived out in the book of Acts. When you share this with your friends in your own words, the power will be present to transform their lives. This message is what brought the power! Let's continue to understand what the Bible says.

> Then Jesus said to His disciples, "Assuredly, I say to you that it is hard for a rich man to enter the <u>kingdom of heaven</u>. And again I say to you, it is easier for a camel to go through the eye of a needle than for a rich man to enter the <u>kingdom of God</u>." (Matt 19:23-4)

> Jesus answered, "<u>My kingdom</u> is not of this world. If <u>My kingdom</u> were of this world, My servants would fight, so that I should not be delivered to the Jews; but now <u>My kingdom</u> is not from here." (John 18:36)

> "And indeed, now I know that you all, among whom I have gone <u>preaching the kingdom of God</u>, will see my face no more. (Acts 20:25)

> So when they had appointed him a day, many came to him at *his* lodging, to whom he explained and solemnly testified of <u>the kingdom of God</u>, persuading them concerning Jesus from both the Law of Moses and the Prophets, from morning till evening. (Acts 28:23)

All these are examples of Jesus and the disciples preaching the Kingdom of God. I am here to tell you that is what Christianity is all about. There is more to this world than meets the eye. We were created as people for fellowship with God. He gave us full reign of the earth as we see in the book of Genesis, but we lost that reign through sin. Humanity, in Adam, committed high treason and gave the reign of this world over to Satan. Jesus came and took the authority back and has given that authority to reign even on this earth to those who believe in Him. It is scriptural. We need to tap into the power Christ has made available to us. This is why kingdom of God people overcome! We are overcomers!

The people in Jesus' day believed that Jesus was going to rule naturally on the earth as a king. What He came to do was to bring back to us as people the ability to be in the kingdom of heaven. The kingdom of heaven and the kingdom of God are synonyms.

His kingdom is a spiritual kingdom that holds up all that is and ever will be. If we are not in His kingdom, we are not in the kingdom of light that will stand forever. His kingdom stands beyond what we see, holds together what we see, and affects all we experience tangibly on this earth. His kingdom supersedes all that we know in our flesh and this is why He can grant us power to reign even while we are here on this earth.

> For if by the one man's offense death reigned through the one, much more those who receive abundance of grace and of the gift of righteousness will <u>reign in life</u> through the One, Jesus Christ. (Romans 5:17)

> Now after John was put in prison, Jesus came to Galilee, preaching the gospel of the kingdom of God, and saying, "The time is fulfilled, <u>and the kingdom of God is at hand</u>. Repent, and believe in the gospel." (Mark 1:14-15)

Hold out for the gospel- don't dilute it. When you stand up and declare it, you will have God's kingdom blessings on this earth. If you dilute it with fear and tradition, you will lose the power in it! When we take our eyes off of ourselves and focus on Jesus then His power is present. Don't worry about having some well-prepared lofty and ideological argument to debate. This is not debate. This is preaching. You are called to proclaim the good news of the Kingdom of God. You get to tell people they don't have to put up with life like that. God has a better way. When you stick to the gospel of the Kingdom you will have demonstration. When you have fear and tradition and man-pleasing, you will lose the power. Rely on God. He is the only one with the power to back up the message.

> For I determined not to know anything among you except Jesus Christ and Him crucified. I was with you in weakness, in fear, and in much trembling. And my speech and my preaching *were* not with persuasive words of human wisdom, but in demonstration of the Spirit and of power, that your faith should not be in the wisdom of men but in the power of God. (I Corinthians 2:2-5)

> Making the word of God of no effect through your tradition which you have handed down. And many such things you do." (Mark 7:13)

I have heard some people say that I wish I could get people healed. I wish I had more of the power of God working through my life. I wish I had more demonstration like Paul had. They think if they could just preach more eloquently that would happen. This is not at all true. It's not about eloquence, it is about the good news you are sharing. Let me ask you a question. Are you sharing healing as a part of the message when you are telling people about Jesus or are you just focusing on salvation? Salvation is obviously the biggest focus, but it is not the only benefit in the kingdom of God. A person cannot have faith for what they have not heard because they don't even know it's a possibility. A person cannot hear without a preacher. You are the preacher. Include this in your conversation and declare this as well. Then step out and pray for them and when they receive Christ, they will be healed as well. The power is in the good news and not eloquence.

7

Where's Your Fishing Hole?

I love to fish. Let me take that back. I love to catch! Some people fish. I catch. People go fishing in many different ways. Some people's idea of fishing is to go out on a boat, plunk a worm into the water, and sit for hours staring at a bobber in hopes a fish gets hungry and tries to take off with their worm. Then, they bring that fish into the boat. Other people pull up a lawn chair on the edge of a lake, sit and wait. They are hoping that a fish will happen to swim by their bait, be attracted to it, and take a bite. In my opinion, this is a slow and boring way to fish. I know that some people want the slow and boring way to fish. They want this because they are really looking for an excuse to take a nap. Well, good for you. Take a nap and get on with your life.

I love to catch. My style of fishing is to go where the fish are and where the fish are biting. I don't want to spend all day sitting in the heat just hoping by chance some fish is going to swim by and take a liking to my worm. I want action. I want results. I want adventure. I will wade the stream, change approaches, and do what's necessary to catch fish. For me, this means I fish with a moving lure that I throw right in where the fish are most likely to be biting. My bait that I throw draws some attention and causes a reaction. Believe me, the reaction is good. I don't want to waste hours. I want to be productive. I enjoy catching fish and I enjoy the great outdoors, but I don't enjoy sitting under the heat of the sun, sweating in a lawn chair, and waiting for a lucky moment. I treasure the adventure in fishing.

I go to where the fish are! I go to where the fish are hungry. I go when the fish are biting. Sometimes this time may be a little inconvenient for me, but the fish are only hungry at certain times. If I want to catch fish and be most successful, I go when and where they are biting. I fish with the bait that they are currently hungry for.

> Walking along the beach of Lake Galilee, Jesus said to them, "Come with me. I'll make a new kind of fisherman out of you. I'll show you how to catch men and women instead of perch and bass." They didn't ask questions, but simply dropped their nets and followed. (Matthew 4:18-20 MSG)

God has called us to catch men and women. He has called us not just to fish, but to catch. Some people have spent years sitting on the side of the lake and thinking they were fishing. Successful fishing is catching. Successful fishing for people catches people for the Kingdom of God. It is God's will that we apply ourselves to be better fishermen and better fisherwomen for God. That is what Invitality is all about.

Even unskilled fishermen get lucky sometimes and maybe this has been your results. Maybe you thought the results that you were getting sharing Christ with people were the norm. Maybe they are the norm around you. God's will is that we go where the fish are, fish with the right bait, and catch them like crazy. That is when fishing is fun. If you are going to be a disciple of Jesus, you are going to be a fisher of men.

If you never go near the water, if you never get out some bait, or if you never go out to fish, then you will have 100% success rate at NOT catching fish. In fact, according to the Word of God, you will be living in the perfect will of the devil for your life. Did I just say that? Yes! God's will is that we go into all the world and preach the gospel. If you never go, if you never share, if you never testify, and you don't plan on it, then you are planning on being in the will of the devil for your life. The devil has a perfect will for you. He can't get you out of the Kingdom of God, so he is going to do all he can to shut you up.

The enemy comes to you and says "You don't know enough." You aren't going to get it right. You better go to church more so you can figure it all out. You can't do it perfectly yet. I am here to tell you that you will not do it perfectly. You are not Jesus. We do the best that we can do with God's help and His grace and mercy makes up the difference. You have to get out of sitting still and go where the fish are. Throw something in the water and get started. You don't have to have it figured out to perfection. Just be you.

If you don't have anything to say to these people, share this. Notice how Paul wrote in this instance more about the glory of God than he did about the past problems he had. Give glory to God and to His Son Jesus. We could say, "I was a jerk to God and was hurting myself and others, but God who loves everyone reached out to me. I received the Truth about Jesus and my sin has been taken away. I can actually know my purpose and enjoy life fulfilled. Does that sound good to you?"

> *You are called to be a catcher of men and I am excited to see you get out there and get results.*

Where is your fishing hole? This is huge. Who are you called to reach? Who are you not called to reach? I know that we all are to live a lifestyle of *Invitality* and to live open to all, but we each have a specific sphere of influence. There are all sorts of fish in a lake, but I am not purposing to catch certain ones. Now if by chance one takes a bite, I will reel it in. In general, we are catching men and women. Specifically, *who* are you fishing for?

This is scriptural. Paul was an apostle called by God and was open to all people, but specifically he was commissioned to reach the Gentiles. Peter was one of the original twelve apostles and loved all people, but he was specifically commissioned to reach the Jews. You are a believer in Jesus. You are called to go and compel all people, but specifically who are you called to compel to come into your life, into church, and into Christ. We need to understand that God has called us to catch men and women and bring them back into relationship with the Father. This process of bringing people back into relationship with God is called *reconciliation*. Every believer has been given the ministry of reconciliation.

> Now all things are of God, who has reconciled us to Himself through Jesus Christ, and has given us the ministry of reconciliation. (2 Corinthians 5:18)

Reconcile means to bring people together. It means to make things right. It means to make a situation righteous. It means to bring people back to God through Christ (Vines, 2013). We live in a world where divorce is rampant. People cite, as a reason for their divorce, the official term "irreconcilable differences." Before accepting Christ, believers are separated from God. They don't have a sin problem. They have an unbelief problem. God sent Jesus to reconcile the irreconcilable differences between Him and humanity.

> "This is how much God loved the world: He gave His Son, his one and only Son. And this is why: so that no one need be destroyed; by believing in him, anyone can have a whole and lasting life. God didn't go to all the trouble of sending his Son merely to point an accusing finger, telling the world how bad it was. He came to help, to put the world right again. Anyone who trusts in Him is acquitted; anyone who refuses to trust him has long since been under the death sentence without knowing it. And why? <u>Because of that person's failure to believe in the one-of-a-kind Son of God when introduced to him</u>. (John 3:16-18 MSG)

Humanity's sin is already paid for through Christ once and for all. It is a completed and signed covenant business deal on God's end. The sin issue has been dealt with, but the unbeliever must accept the payment to have their balance sheet reconciled. The only way this happens is through believing in Jesus and confessing Him as Lord. We don't rid their sin. God already paid the price to do that. We rid their disbelief. His payment was enough to cover all their debt, so we just let people know that any sin that would hold them back has been paid for. They are free to receive eternal life and fellowship with God. Just trust and call on Jesus as your Lord and the payment is released unto your account.

We are called to recognize the unbelievers that are in our sphere of influence and reconcile them to God. This is what I am referring to as "catching men." Who are the fish you are called to reach?

It's so easy to catch fish if we go to where the fish are. We don't go fishing in a pool. We don't go fishing in the boat. We don't go fishing in a sewer system. Why? The fish are in the streams, rivers, ponds, lakes, and oceans. They typically like a certain habitat in those bodies of water. People spend all sorts of money buying equipment that they can use to spot fish under and in the water. They want to get out there in the water and put their boat right on top of where the fish are located. Are you starting to get my point? You have to figure out who you are called to reach and where?

Where is your fishing hole? For most people this is the group of people you are around in your sphere of influence. You have family close to you, you have friends close to you, and you have coworkers close to you. You may even volunteer in a community organization. This is your sphere of influence. Specifically, this is your primary fishing hole!

It is time for you to look at your fishing hole through God's eyes. We can no longer sit in the boat (at church) week after week and ignore all the hungry fish we are with during the week. Jesus said the harvest is plentiful and the laborers are few. I say the harvest is plentiful, get out of the pew! Think right now of people in your family, your friendship circle, and your workplace who don't know Jesus. Stop and ask God right now to help you reach them.

I want to encourage you to keep things simple. I love how Phillip reached someone for Christ in the book of Acts. We can look at his example of reaching someone through *Invitality* with the gospel of the Kingdom of God. Then, we can take this as our example and follow easy steps to catch men.

Now an angel of the Lord spoke to Philip, saying, "Arise and go toward the south along the road which goes down from Jerusalem to Gaza." This is desert. So he arose and went. And behold, a man of Ethiopia, a eunuch of great authority under Candace the queen of the Ethiopians, who had charge of all her treasury, and had come to Jerusalem to worship, was returning. And sitting in his chariot, he was reading Isaiah the prophet. Then the Spirit said to Philip, "Go near and overtake this chariot."

So Philip ran to him, and heard him reading the prophet Isaiah, and said, "Do you understand what you are reading?"

And he said, "How can I, unless someone guides me?" And he asked Philip to come up and sit with him. The place in the Scripture which he read was this:

> "He was led as a sheep to the slaughter;
> And as a lamb before its shearer *is* silent,
> So He opened not His mouth.
> In His humiliation His justice was taken away,
> And who will declare His generation?
> For His life is taken from the earth."

So the eunuch answered Philip and said, "I ask you, of whom does the prophet say this, of himself or of some other man?" Then Philip opened his mouth, and beginning at this Scripture, preached Jesus to him. Now as they went down the road, they came to some water. And the eunuch said, "See, *here is* water. What hinders me from being baptized?"

> Then Philip said, "If you believe with all your heart, you may."

> And he answered and said, "I believe that Jesus Christ is the Son of God."
>
> So he commanded the chariot to stand still. And both Philip and the eunuch went down into the water, and he baptized him. (Acts 8: 26-38)

I want you to notice these things about Philip's experience and how they speak to us today. First, recognize sharing the gospel is supernatural. We must position ourselves to be led by the Spirit of God. In this case, an angel of the Lord spoke to Philip and gave him directions. We are not to seek angels. We are to seek God. If He chooses to speak to us through spectacular or different means like an angel or dream that is great, but in general, we receive direction from the Bible and by the Holy Spirit in our heart bearing witness to us. The Spirit of God will give us intuitions of where we need to be at certain times. For example, you may currently use your lunch break at work to get away from everyone and read your Bible. If you are open to the leading of the Holy Spirit, He may lead you to go to the break room where someone is going to come in for a conversation. Remember, choosing to live this lifestyle of *Invitality* is worship unto God. It could mean the difference in someone's eternal destiny.

Second, ask a question. You will notice from the account that Philip became aware of the surroundings and then asked "Do you understand what you are reading?" Asking a question controls the direction a conversation is going. Remember, we have a goal in mind with our question. The goal is to catch people. If you will learn to ask good questions, your chance to share the goodness of God will increase dramatically. Notice he did not ask the man from Ethiopia about his lifestyle. He asked Him something pertaining to understanding. If we ask questions about lifestyle it often causes walls to come up in conversation. He also did not ask him what he thought about some distant philosophical thing. Even though he was reading scripture, Philip focused the question on the individual. We must do the same. Jesus is about that person. We are about reaching that person, not about changing their whole way of thinking about life in one conversation.

Third and very important, wait and listen. Actively listen to what the person is saying. Listen with your heart, mind, soul, and strength. Look them in the eye to show you care, but relax. The way you listen allows them to bare their heart to you. Listen with gracious sensitivity. You are showing the compassion of Christ. You may not agree with what they say. You are not called to be the agreement police. You are called to invite people into your life, into church, and into Christ. Open wide the gate of salvation. We open wide the gate for others to explore faith in Christ by the way we listen. Listen with your spirit and look for an opportunity to share. Don't interrupt unless they are a talker and will just keep going forever. We will spend time on recognizing the open door in another chapter.

Fourth, when you sense the opportunity to share, starting with where the person is at in conversation, share your personal testimony. I don't mean get up on a chair in the break room with a microphone and a keyboard player and give an altar call. I mean share from your heart your testimony of what good thing God has done for you as it related to them. Speak like a real person. Share from your heart. Try not to use biblical words that only Christians would understand. Don't say "Jesus was the *propitiation* for my sin." You will have to define the term *propitiation* and that will bring confusion. Just keep your message simple and real about what Jesus has done for you. Say something like "I can understand your perspective. Let me share with you what I have experienced because of Jesus in my life." Do this with tact. We will cover this elsewhere in the book.

Finally, give them an opportunity to receive what you are offering them- Jesus! "This is what Jesus has done for me and He will do the same thing for you. Would you like to receive Him today?" Putting the decision in their control values them as an individual and lets them tell you if they are ready. This is such an important part of catching men. I am always amazed when I talk to people how many have heard things about Jesus before, but were never given an opportunity to receive salvation for themselves. If you are asking a question and then sharing a testimony about Jesus, the Holy Spirit is going to convict and open a door for salvation. Don't stop short. Just ask the question and you will be amazed at the work God has done through your testimony. Pray the salvation prayer right then and there.

I will also mention this. It is not kind to birth a baby into the world and not take care of nurturing it. Please plan to follow up with your newborn Christian and get them into church. Get them into a new believer's class. Attend it with them if at all possible. Support them and introduce them to new friends in the church. Invite them into your social circle or help them find a Christian one of their own. We want a victorious life not just a victorious moment.

Now let's get back to our fishing example.

A fisherman finds a spot where there is fish he wants to reach. Then he puts his bait on to catch fish. What is your bait? Your bait is the relevant question that you will ask your coworkers to open a door to their heart. Go to work and listen to people talk. Listen to God on the inside of you and allow Him to give you a question to ask. When the question that you will ask works properly, your personal testimony of something good God has done for you fits right into conversation. The most recent report of God's goodness seems to work best. I suppose you can catch a fish on an old worm, but the livelier ones attract more attention. The truth is most people are unprepared for an opportunity to share Christ because they haven't sat back in this busy world and taken account of the good things God is doing right now in their lives. They have not looked at their workplace, their school board, their family and asked God for a question that could open doors to conversation and salvation. Stop right here and think about what your question may be. You must prepare to catch fish. If your question is not working to open the door after a couple months, change your question.

The goal of the question we are asking is to open the door to a conversation where we can bring it back to Jesus. If your question simply leads to philosophical thought and not real life experience, I would suggest changing questions. Jesus is the pivotal point in the conversation. Also, please remember that you are in relationship with these people on a regular basis. God may lead you through a series of questions over days or weeks in order to open the door for your testimony. In general, though, I have found that most people slow the process down by their own fear to pursue catching men and not out of someone being closed off to the gospel.

Fishermen cast bait out one way and get no bite. Then, cast out bait several other ways and still get no bite. A casual fisherman just sits there and keeps casting. Stop it! You are no longer a casual fisherman. You are not a casual Christian. You are a believer with a lifestyle of Invitality. You are purposely inviting people into your life, into church, and into Christ. Without results, something needs to change.

A good fisherman adjusts to the fishing environment. If the fish aren't biting on the first bait, he doesn't just keep going. He pulls in the line and puts on something else. His goal is not to throw stuff in the water. His goal is to get bites and catch fish. If what you have been doing isn't getting bites, let's stop and ask a question. Who are you trying to reach? What is the right bait? Different fish bite on different things. If you are called to reach them, be yourself but change your approach.

When fishing for people you are going to be in the outdoors. It may get a little adventurous. I have found most people treat the sharing of their faith like how they take care of a classic car. A classic car owner takes such good care of that car. They wash the car far more than they actually show the car. They want that car to be prim, proper, and shiny. In general, they keep the car covered and in the garage. When they take the car out they don't want to get a smudge from a bug on that car. They are so concerned with it being clean and pretty that they don't even drive through certain neighborhoods. As the church, we are not classic cars. We need to quit being preoccupied with cleaning ourselves up to perfection. We need to get out of being in church constantly and get out where the fish are. Fish are in the water and not in the boat. You may get wet. You will come in contact with dirt, but thank God the Word of God washes us clean. We need to take the glory of God to work, to our family, and to our friends.

These same principles apply to personal fishing and also for corporate fishing. Corporate fishermen reach masses of fish, so they don't fish with a single line. They fish with nets. They still use bait and go to where the fish are located, but they drop nets. They go through the seas and drop the nets to depths where the fish are located. They don't just leave their boat in the bay and say "here, fishy-fishy."

The corporate fisherman is the local church. The local church is called to reach the harvest. Each local church is called to be reaching fish in mass. The local church needs to go through the same process of asking where is our fishing hole? The local church needs to ask the question what is our bait? What question are we trying to put out there to a group of people and then answer with God's goodness for them?

There is a personal side to evangelism. We are all called to be ministers of reconciliation. But there is also a corporate side that we are involved with through our local church. Each person is to have a part in both. Some people are stopped from personal evangelism because they get their focus on an ocean of people they are trying to reach. Churches are called to oceans, evangelists are called to oceans, and missionaries may be called to oceans. Most people are called to reach people right in their sphere of influence. Love and give to reach the masses, but focus your energies and prayers on reaching your personal fishing hole. What question can you ask that one person at your workplace to open the heart and open the door for your testimony? I hope that you are getting a revelation on *Invitality* and how it can be applied into your life.

One must understand that in regards to sharing Jesus effectively, questions are the answer.

Do you see that through living a lifestyle of *Invitality* we ask questions? Questions value the other individual as precious in God's sight. They are the practical way that we invite others into our lives, and then we can invite them to Christ! Questions open doors to the spirit of a person and where they are at in life.

8

Invitality = Church Growth

This book is written to both believers and leaders in the body of Christ. I would be remiss not to explain to you the results that Invitality has for growth of the local church. I believe that God is using the local churches all around the world to reach people in masses and we have only seen the beginning. God wants his local churches full of believers that are growing spiritually and sharing enthusiastically.

I don't know of one pastor in his/her right mind who doesn't want the church to grow. I don't know of one believer in Jesus Christ with their mind renewed to the Word of God who doesn't want the church to grow. Anything that is healthy is growing. Now, it may be growing smarter or it may be growing taller or it may be growing stronger, but it is growing. Kids that are healthy grow! Corporations that are healthy grow. Churches that are healthy grow! I don't want you to think of your church as a good church or bad church. I want you to think of your church in regards to its health. Healthy churches grow.

This chapter dives into strategy and shares that *Invitality* works! I have proven it out in the local church and can now share this message with you. This chapter is the background of how God got this message of Invitality over to our local church and the results that we have experienced. My prayer is that the word God has shared with us would become alive to you and that you would experience even greater results.

Seeds of the *Invitality* movement actually began in the 1990's through a vision that God showed our lead pastor. The vision is recorded for you just how he tells it. Please understand that we are not led first by visions. We are led first by the Word of God. The Bible says that we are to go out and compel others to come in. That is enough for us all. However, in this case, God saw fit to help us catch *Invitality* by sharing a couple of visions with pastors. I think God is very serious about His harvest and is trying to get people to listen.

The Harvest Vision

> A number of years ago, we had an evangelist named David Egli come minister here at the church. (We've known David and his wife, Linda, for many years. Who they are in the Lord and how they lived their lives had a *huge* impact on us in the early years of our Christian lives and ministry.)
>
> In the course of his message that day, David looked at me and said, "Loren, (we're close enough friends that he calls me by my first name,) "in all the churches where I've ministered, I've *never been in one* that had a revelation of the Great Commission."

I was sitting in the front row, and when he said that my lips and my tongue began to burn, and I saw a vision—

I saw a farmstead, I saw the farmhouse—two stories with an attic, a tall, typical white, wood-sided farmhouse, with a gravel driveway coming north off the road that ran along the south side of the lawn, going down past the east side of the house to the outbuildings (the garage, machine shed, the lots and the buildings for the livestock)…and, there were fields all around.

I saw people standing out on the lawn—like they'd gathered and had been waiting for something--a lot of people, not just a few, the lawn was pretty well full of people.

I saw flatbed semis, semi-tractors pulling flatbed trailers into the driveway, carrying harvest equipment—combines and heads.

And I heard the Lord say, "The harvest crew is arriving, yet not exactly. They're arriving from the manufacturer, delivering harvest equipment; and they'll be harvesting--harvesting and training these standing around in harvesting."

And He made me to know that the Manufacturer of the equipment was also the owner of the farm, of these fields—<u>and that these standing around were not just laborers, but were actually newly-hired factory representatives who would be</u>

> trained in harvesting. They'd be trained and they'd be harvesting…and then *they* would go out and deliver harvest equipment, harvest and train in harvesting and then *those in turn* would go out, deliver equipment, harvest and train in harvesting…and on and on.

And that's what this church is all about.

Now, let me explain to you what is going on in this vision. Visions show pictures and the pictures represent things. In this vision, the harvest represents people. These are the people that need to be reached with the message of the Kingdom of God. "Training in harvesting" refers to people discipled to understand the basics of the Christian faith, their gifting given by God, and especially the believer's call to evangelism. "Go out and deliver harvest equipment, harvest, and train in harvesting and on and on" means there is to be a continual expansion of believers doing the work of evangelism. It also means that those called to be pastors, teachers, apostles, prophets, and evangelists will be equipping the saints to go launch other works. Not every believer will be delivering harvest equipment and training, but all will be bringing in the harvest.

Once this vision was explained to the people, the church had a mural of a harvest field painted in the sanctuary, prayer continued, the Word of God was taught, and a Bible school was started. These are all great things and were steps forward, but the church did not grow in any significant number.

I was not at the church for several years in the 1990's because I was attending college. You will remember that I started this book telling you about my experience at Iowa State University. God was opening my heart to the plight of humanity and placing within me a call to pour out His love to people. After my college years, my wife and I made our way back to serve in the local church. Most of my life I have had a desire to see people come to know Jesus. I was a "good" Christian. I had led people to Christ, but these experiences were few and far between. Every church I was involved with had about the same results in their services.

The vision from God was delivered to the lead pastor. The lead pastor was interested in getting results. He wanted more. I wanted more. Everyone wanted more. We wanted to reach the lost. Desire is so important to our ability to grow. Our church had a desire to see people come to know Jesus. Our whole church leadership was praying for an increase in people coming to know Jesus through the ministry. I remember this year clearly because for the first time ever, our lead pastor stood up before the membership and said that we were going to shoot for having sixty people come to know Jesus directly through our Sunday morning service for the year.

We prayed together as leadership and as a congregation and asked God for sixty salvations in our Sunday morning ministry. We wanted to allow God to use us to reach the lost, but I learned that desire alone is not enough. Desire can catapult you out of the gate with fire, but purposeful strategy helps you stay the course to a desired end. At the end of that year we had less than thirty confirmed salvations in our Sunday morning service. Now I say confirmed because you can't track people that don't fill out information or for which you have no tangible record. There are all sorts of ways to track information, but I am not getting into that here. (You can contact my ministry for coaching if this interests you). Now, there were other salvations in other departments of the ministry throughout the church, but no one was satisfied. The Lead Pastor wasn't satisfied, people weren't satisfied, and I believe God wasn't satisfied with our results. It was frustrating, but the answer is not to fire a growing leadership team. The answer is to take these results back to God, get counsel, and face the facts. Now, I have come to believe that God allowed us to form a goal knowing that we would not meet it that first year. Why? God needed our ministry to face the facts regarding our programs and our personal lifestyles.

We faced the facts. Since we still believed it was God's will to use our Sunday morning service to reach the lost, we were going to have to change things going on in the Sunday morning service. We were not going to water down the message of salvation or stop preaching the Word of God. We did decide to be much more intentional about what was in and not in a Sunday morning service. We decided on our Sunday morning service "negotiable" and "non-negotiable" items. Then, with the help of the Holy Spirit, we set new goals and began to track our success in reaching them. We have purposefully adjusted programs and goals and are experiencing better results. Understand that you never stop tweaking for success, but when you clarify the mission of what you are trying to accomplish in a given service, it allows you some parameters to tweak within and brings much peace down the road when confronted with new ideas, philosophies, and approaches.

That's when it happened. I was in prayer during the early summer of 2011. I was calling out to God for help. We desperately wanted to reach the lost and we were willing to change. I was willing to change. God heard my cry and gave me a vision in prayer. This was not the same type of vision as the Lead Pastor. He had what is known as an open vision. His eyes were open, but he saw into another place. I had my eyes closed and was praying when it came. In order to best understand what this vision is about you may want to know what a harvesting combine is. A combine is a huge piece of farming equipment kind of like a tractor but much cooler!

They are used by farmers to harvest grain out of their fields. Combines are very expensive and are getting more and more efficient at their role each year. The name *combine* derives from its combining of three separate harvesting operations- reaping, threshing, and winnowing in one machine. A harvest combine has something called a "head" out on the front of them that reaps the grain. So, in the case of harvesting corn, the combine can actually pick the corn plant, shuck all husk from the corn, take the corn off the cob, and then shoot it into a storage silo for drying. Wow! You have to love technology. That is one productive piece of equipment. Understanding what a combine is helps you to understand the vision that God showed me as I prayed for the lost in my city. Here is what I saw.

The Combine Vision

> I saw a beautiful combine. It was state of the art with all the bells and whistles. The combine was *John Deere* green. It was all shined up and ready to bring in the harvest. There was a driver in the combine and all of the attachments to bring in the harvest were linked onto the machine. It was a beautiful piece of machinery sparkling in the sunshine. I'm telling you it was sharp! The Lord said to me "Isn't that a good-lookin combine?" I spoke back to Him in the vision "that *is* a great looking combine, Lord." As I continued to pray, the picture of what I saw opened wider and that beautiful combine was actually driving down the highway. Then God showed me as the combine

was driving down the highway, that the combine was in great shape, it was totally full of gas, and ready. I even saw people looking on from afar pointing and saying "wow, look at that good looking combine!"

Then God said to me "that great, green combine is actually one *sad* combine." I felt devastated more than I can explain in words and I didn't understand why it was a sad combine. My eyes teared up as I prayed. He then showed me that the combine keeps getting all cleaned up, getting all filled up through revivals, and just keeps going down the highway. Then someone cleans it up again and someone fuels it up again and it just keeps going down the highway. It's good to get cleaned up. It's good to get filled up. But a combine is not meant for the highway. It finds its greatest joy by turning aside into a specific field and reaping the harvest."

When He said this to me, the meaning of this vision hit me like a ton of bricks. The great, green, shiny harvest combine was actually the Church! There is a time to get cleaned up from our sin. There is a time to be refueled with the Holy Spirit, but the Church is meant to be a harvesting machine. A harvesting machine is to purposely get filled up and cleaned up to reach a specific harvest field. I saw a sad combine that kept going down the highway until it got a little dirty and ran out of gas. Then, they would fill the tank up through revival and the combine would keep going down the highway. The harvest combine looked pretty on the outside, but on the inside it was void of fulfillment and it was sad!

I believe this vision that God gave me is supernaturally attached to the one He gave the lead pastor of our local church. I actually went and shared with him the vision and asked him for his input. It is a good idea, when we receive direction in prayer, to seek out our spiritual authority and get feedback. Our spiritual authorities are no substitute for the Bible, Jesus, or the Holy Spirit, but often they are able to tell us if we are "missing it" in regards to our understanding.

It turns out that what I saw in the vision "lined up" with what our lead pastor had experienced from God years earlier. The color of the tractors was the same, the call to reach the harvest was the same, the witness of the Holy Spirit was present in both of our hearts, and it was not contrary to the written scriptures. We both saw the harvest fields that needed to be reached. God is the same yesterday, today, and forever. He is trying His hardest to get every church out there reaping and in this case showed visions to two persons in leadership to get the church out there into the harvest field!

I need you to understand this. Each individual member of the body of Christ is a harvester. Each of us is a person out there in a field harvesting wheat with a sickle. A sickle is an effective tool for one person to harvest a small field. You can reach certain areas individually that a massive machine cannot reach.

> *The church, on the other hand, is a huge group of people and it is more like a combine.*

When all the parts work together as they should, each one with their gifts, the potential to reach the masses is huge. You have people with evangelistic gifts, people with teaching gifts, giving gifts, hospitality gifts, mercy gifts…etc. All the gifts work together in tandem. We all are supposed to reach the lost in our fishing hole, but as part of the church combine we have a specific part to play to reach the masses.

Here is how the combine vision applies both to individuals and to churches. People come to church and give their lives to Christ and start to get cleaned up from their sin. Then, they enjoy special meetings, revivals, and special worship services and get all filled up with the Holy Spirit. They are amped up for something, but they don't realize the purpose of getting cleaned up and filled up. So they just live life like usual slowly becoming downtrodden from life experiences and looking for the next special service, special book, new music release, or whatever to give them a quick fix revival. But all along, they were set free and revived for a purpose: to turn aside into a new lifestyle and reach the harvest right where they live! When they don't do this, they may look and feel good for a little bit, but their inner fulfillment and joy is lacking. Soon, their filling runs out and they begin to talk bad about the filling station- church and God. The problem is not necessarily the filling station. The problem is what they are doing in their lives once they are filled.

Here is an application for local churches. In churches and church leadership circles, the tendency is to serve the people and the immediate needs that are right in front of them. This is good as long as there is a balance. Here is what happens: Church leaders (whom I honor, by the way) put together special programs and meetings and awesome ministry takes place. I want you to know that pastors and church leaders can really put together some awesome ministry for people. The church overall gets cleaned up from sin and lethargy, and new momentum is infused into the congregation. The church is revived! People are actually walking in love again with one another and the spiritual gifts are flowing in the congregation. What happens next is the point of the vision. If the church continues simply in this flow, it will become sad! Frustration will come and set in once again. This is one of the reasons that churches get stuck at a certain size and can't break through growth barriers. They are stuck in this cycle. The church must realize its single biggest mandate! The church that is cleaned up and filled up must strategically turn aside into the harvest field. A happy combine is a harvesting combine. A happy church is a harvesting church. There is a time for cleaning up. There is a time for filling up. Now, is the time to harvest!

Since having this vision in prayer I have come to see the importance of the driver of that combine. I have also come to see the magnitude of strategically turning aside into the harvest field. This means that the pastor must have a heart for the harvest and must allow the church to come up with a plan! The pastor does not have to have the plan. The pastor can have a plan, but it doesn't have to come that way. A plan could come through prayer, laymen, evangelists, consultants, or any number of ways. The pastor simply has to have a big enough heart for the harvest that he/she opens the door for planning. If you are in a church that does not have *a written plan* to reach the harvest, this is a word from God to you. Under the authority of and most likely with the local pastor, I would encourage you to get some strategic prayer and planning going and do it without delay.

I would also encourage you to honor your pastor, your driver. You may work together to strategically plan, but in the local church, the pastor must hear the Word from God to turn aside into a ripe field. At some point, the pastor must sit up in the chair of that combine and point over there to a field and say "that's the one...that's the way...let's turn aside to that one." Don't pressure your pastor. Honor your pastor. Don't hinder your driver. Help your driver to say "yes...that's who we need to go after. Now, go ahead and make it happen." Your pastor is to guide you into greener pastures. He/she has a gift from God to do this. They will listen to your advice, but in the end God will show them the right timing to turn aside into the field. I say this with humility, boldness and tenacity.

God can NOT bless a church without a harvest plan!

This message of *Invitality* is not something that happens separate from the local church. A church has goals, but a church is made up of people. People are the church and without the people grabbing onto the vision and moving together into the harvest field there will be no change. Now culture in a church can be confronted from the lay people upward, but the culture changing comes from the top of the organization down. If you want to see epic results in your church, it is not enough for a specific few individuals to grab onto Invitality and run with it. There must be pastoral buy-in. At some point, the pastor must have a heart for the lost. Most do. Otherwise, they wouldn't have started in ministry. However, it is easy to lose sight of what is going on out in the battlefield when you are in the ER bandaging up the broken. As a pastor, when you are dealing with family issues, marriages, divorces, funerals, counseling, budgets, attitudes, outright sin, as well as bills and boards, it is easy to lose focus and energy for what's important.

Please understand that I am not telling any pastor what to do. A pastor sees the needs of the congregation and brings them beside the still waters and into green pastures. He leads them into security and fulfillment in God. He needs to be led by God when to launch into something new as a church and when to say to the people "that's a good idea, but not this year." God allows pastors to sense timing. The pastor doesn't have to have the whole plan, but he/she needs to be able to commission the plan brought to him.

The pastor seeks God, stands in the gap for the people, and has their best in mind. A pastor is a gift from God to serve a people and is to be honored. When a people honor their pastor, they are honoring God, and God can bring blessing to them. If they think they know it all and are going to tell their pastor how he/she should run the church and how he/she is missing it here and there, they need to read the story in scripture of when the people complained against Moses. You can have an open conversation with your pastor when he/she opens his/her heart to you. This comes by building trust with them. They need to know that you have their back and aren't stabbing them in the back. If you have a history of being the backstabber, then this process is going to take time. Trust is built. Trust is the roadway for the acceptance of new thoughts and ideas. Help your leader to trust your heart for them before ever trying to change things. You may think that God has called you to be a change agent. Then my word to you is that God has first called you to be a trust-building agent.

Let me get back to turning aside into your harvest field. Personally, each individual has a harvest field. This is made up of the areas where you spend most of your time. Have you considered your harvest field as a church? The local church is to be reaching a harvest field. The local church is to be a corporate harvesting machine. Each harvesting machine, known as a combine, is meant to work in a field. But you don't take your combine and just run it in any field that you feel like it and have success. Can you imagine pulling your combine into a field that was not yours and starting to just drive all over in circles without a plan? Can you imagine the chaos that would ensue if your teenage son got in your combine one day and drove 3 farms away and decided to plow the field in such a way as to draw figurines that were noticeable from the sky? I think this is hilarious, but I doubt most people would. Keep in mind this is in someone else's field. I am here to tell you people would be chasing you down and going nuts! They don't care if it looks like Mickey Mouse from the sky and is a perfect rendition. It is wrong! If you know farmers and farm country, it would spread like wild-fire. The event would never go away. It would be "the talk" from every gas station to breakfast bar. It would be on the farm report and the local news. Why? Someone got out of their place. The son didn't stay in his role. He went renegade.

Every local church is to be a harvesting machine. We are all to be reaching the harvest in a general sense. However, strategically and specifically, what field has God sent your church to reach this year? Your harvest fields may change from time to time. You may grow in your ability to harvest multiple fields over time at the same time, but a harvesting operation starts with a clarified purpose.

Who is your church specifically trying to reach with the gospel of Jesus Christ?

When you answer this question as a leadership team, it will help you to set your goals. Then, you can minister to the people in such a way that they latch onto the vision and accomplish it. They will be satisfied and God will be honored! If you shoot to accomplish "whatever," you will get it every time, and it means very little difference made for the Kingdom of God. Churches are at all different stages with strategic planning, leadership structures, and health, but if you are going to reach the lost with exponential increase you must get strategic about it. No church has it all down perfect, but the results of moving this direction are astounding.

How could this impact your church? How could this impact your city? God brought two visions to leaders of our local church and He brought Invitality as the primary way to get people into their harvest field. When this message was birthed in my heart for the body of Christ, the lead pastor opened the door to pour it into the people. He opened up his Sunday pulpit to the message. Then, because of prayer, our lead pastor declared our first strategic harvest field is going to be young families. Immediately things began to change. Check out the corporate results.

The first year of beginning to incorporate this message of Invitality into our local congregation both individually and corporately, <u>we experienced a 20% growth in the church</u>! We made plans and launched another service to reach more of the lost! We set up an outreach event in our city. We also hired a new Children's Pastor.

As a harvesting church, we prayed, planned, and clarified our first harvest field: families with kids. This helped to guide our decisions about finances, building plans, and programs. We turned the harvesting combine into the harvest field known as families. Honoring families has always been a core value at our church, but we felt God wanted us to focus especially on it.

We have a long way to go as a people, but there is tangible momentum in the atmosphere of the church when you walk in the door. People are asking each other "I wonder what new faces we are going to see this week?" People have come to the point of expecting not to know everyone who is sitting in the seats. I rejoice in the growth of the church and in the lives that have been changed so far through the local church adopting a culture of Invitality.

The second year of beginning to incorporate this message of Invitality into our local congregation both individually and corporately, <u>we experienced 75% growth from our original size of the church</u>! Our <u>children's ministry has doubled</u> in size and our <u>youth ministry recorded double the salvations</u> of any other year on record. Isn't salvation and growing a relationship with God what this is all about?

Now, I have some final thoughts on strategically planning to reach the lost. I have mentioned goals. I have mentioned picking a specific harvest field. But the harvesting machine- the church- must take into account the array of people that will now be coming through the doors of your church.

A major error that many churches make is trying to reach all people at all points in their spiritual journey in one ministry environment. If you do this, you will have minimal results and the people will eventually stop inviting. If you do this, you make your ministry into a "melting pot" spiritually. A "melting pot" has all different flavors in it, but not one of them is really effectual. You can't reach people with a super deep message of the Word and not be speaking above the understanding of an unbeliever.

How do you solve this? The answer is to strategically plan different ministry environments to reach specific groups of people. Communicate this to your congregation with heart and passion. Transition the church over a period of months. Current trends for America point out that most people come to church and to Christ for the first time on a Sunday morning. This trend was not the case years ago as most denominations had special meetings in the evenings or tents to reach people far from God. However, it seems to be the trend now. (Reiner, 2003) This causes churches to have to restructure what they are doing on Sunday mornings. Now, growing churches are reaching the lost on Sunday mornings rather than just feeding the sheep. Feeding the sheep is important. We need to grow the new and maturing believers, but we need to create a specific environment to do that. We must set up ministry environments to reach, to raise up, and to release people into their divine destinies. When your church really catches on to *Invitality* your Sunday am service will be your primary service to reach the lost.

It is imperative that you set up a discipleship path for these new converts to follow when they make the decision to be reconciled to God. They are babies spiritually and don't know directions. I firmly believe that when God knows you have a system to disciple new believers in place and begin to make Invitality your church culture, the increase will come. From what I have seen over several different churches all over the country, when you get ready for the explosion, God will bring it.

If you fail to strategically place leaders over areas of discipleship you are choosing to fail. If you think that you will do this ONCE they show up and get saved, you are too late. You will lose the fruit that God can bring your ministry. What smart person would send someone to a college before the college had a curriculum for education. No smart individual would ever settle with that sort of lackadaisical planning in education. What makes us think that God would settle for that in regard to the precious fruit of the earth? When we get our plan for discipleship in place as the Holy Spirit has directed and then launch out into the deep for a catch, God will bring them until our nets are breaking. This means more services, bigger venues, and a whole new set of "problems" to rejoice about. I would rather work through these problems than be asking "why isn't anyone showing up?" I have been on both sides of this and the growing side is better!

Now is the time to apply your faith in planning and praying personally and corporately as a church. We ought to have salvation goals in our personal lives and in the church. We should ask God for His help accomplishing them. You may not have a degree in strategic planning, but you can still seek God and make a goal as to how many people He would like you to reach this year! Make some plans and write them down. You are 80% more likely to accomplish things that you write down.

As church leadership, seek God together and decide on your first harvest field to turn into. Hopefully, you already know your church's overall vision, but what is your specific harvest field for the year? What are your salvation goals for the year as a church? Do you have a way to tabulate your success? Stretch your faith and believe God for increase, because it forces you to rely on God for creative ideas and teamwork. It forces you to rely on His grace, and it forces you to apply graceful works to your faith.

This is when the power of God and that Spirit of faith rises up on the inside of you and causes you to speak to the mountains that have been holding you back.

> For assuredly, I say to you, whoever says to this mountain, 'Be removed and be cast into the sea,' and does not doubt in his heart, but believes that those things he says will be done, he will have whatever he says. Therefore, I say to you, whatever things you ask when you pray, believe that you receive *them*, and you will have *them*. (Mark 11:23-24)

I believe God loves it when we get busy about His harvest and He begins to pour out blessing. The momentum that birthed in our church was amazing and is continuing. That spirit led momentum is open to you and your church. Of course, nothing is possible without prayer, and though people are involved, Jesus gets all the glory.

You may be thinking "I would like some good momentum going on in my church. How do I get it?" Some people sense momentum when it is there. It is like excitement just hanging in the air. Some people sense when momentum is missing. The atmosphere is dead and stagnant. The leader needs to be able to create it. A leader must ask "How can I create some godly momentum?" How can I birth a movement of *Invitality* in my church?

Momentum is created by participating in a series of small wins.

That statement right there took me years to figure out. Momentum is huge and helpful in reaching the lost as a church, but it cannot sustain for any length of time if the leadership doesn't set a strategy that makes room for the sharing of the gospel. Take a step. Make a goal. Gather a team. Launch one prayer-filled outreach. Evaluate. Then set strategy to release the whole church with Invitality. I've heard it said in the church, "We are positioned and poised to grow." That is a great start! I could have a super capable combine and I could take it to the edge of the field, position it there, poised, and ready to harvest. It will never reach its full potential until someone starts the engine and actually gets out there in the harvest field.

You can do this. You belong out there in the field. I believe in you.

9

Practically Speaking

Strategic thinking is typically a long term approach, whereas tactics are for the short term. Tactics are approaches you can change right away to start experiencing success. This chapter is about adopting tactics that work individually for success in reaching people. Along with preaching the right message, *Invitality* takes "connecting" with the person to whom we are speaking. We can count on the Holy Spirit's help in this. Remember, our simple goal is to invite people into our lives, invite them to church, and invite them to Christ. Keeping things simple helps you be yourself. God called you to reach people. He chose you to reach your sphere of influence, so let me give you some advice that will make you successful.

To connect with others, you must have the right mindset about others and about your local church. In regards to daily life be others-focused. A person who is others-focused takes time to pray for the lost. Their prayers are not filled with words like me, my, and mine. It is not that they don't have needs that they are praying for and about, but their needs are not as big as someone else about to die and be in hell. A person that is others-focused recognizes all the different people who make up their daily sphere of influence and looks for opportunities. They open their homes up to be a place of ministry to these people. They recognize when people are missing at work due to illness or when someone's attitude seems off. Here is a recent account of what being other-focused can do.

Bella worked the cashier lane at BigBox-Mart and she noticed that another woman had a job coming into the store and restocking the magazine racks. The woman would come in often and Bella would make a point to talk to her. Each time, Bella would just open up her life to Barb and invite her to church. She was purposely praying and showing God's love. Barb would come by weekly and the two of them became accustomed to interacting. Then something changed. Bella noticed that Barb was gone and not making her regular rounds to stock the magazine racks. They weren't close friends and she didn't have her number, but wondered where she had been.

After a while, Barb showed up again to stock racks and made her way through the store toward Betty's cashier lane. Immediately upon noticing her back in her lane, she told Barb she had missed her. She asked how she had been. It was at this moment that the invitations to church and the friendliness paid off. Barb stopped stocking the magazines in the cashier lane. She looked up and said that her kidneys were failing. She had to take time off because of illness but the company was pressuring her to be at work. Barb then mentioned something that they had talked about in a conversation many visits before. She reminded Bella about her mentioning a "bridge" and that she wanted to know exactly what she meant by it. After a moment of reflection, Bella remembered sharing with her about Jesus being the bridge of salvation.

She began to share again how God loved her and how Jesus was the way of salvation. Right in the check-out isle of BigBox-Mart the woman began to cry. That was not something anyone expected. She thought she should go around the counter and maybe give her a hug. When she started to go around the counter, the line leader of the check-out lines showed up. Bella thought "uh-oh." But what happened next just adds to this being a God moment. Right there in the store, the line leader looked at the woman crying. She reached up and turned off the light for the isle and said "Bella, please take care of your customer." She stared in amazement as the line leader moved on down the check-out lanes. Then she turned back to Barb in the check-out lane and prayed with her to receive salvation! Shortly after that salvation prayer the woman came to church.

Invitation to church comes best after you invite people into your life. In this case, the woman was invited into Bella's life at the cashier lane of BigBox-Mart over several conversations and she invited her to church several times. It just happened in this case that salvation happened in the check-out isle. This may not be the usual case. What is the usual case is that when you invite a person into your life, it makes a way for them to receive salvation either in person or at church. The further follow up to this specific salvation experience is that Barb was healed of her kidney disease in the first service that she came to at the church. We found out three months later that she was able to quit her magazine stocking job and pass a physical exam to go on the road truck-driving with her husband.

A person who is others-focused lives with gracious sensitivity to human failure. They acknowledge that sin is real. They do not ignore that sin is there in someone's life, but they are able to separate the value of the person from the sin they are wrapped up in. They are also willing to put up with the smell of drugs or alcohol in order to show the love of Christ. This doesn't mean someone partakes in something out beyond his/her Christian convictions, but they are willing to put their own feelings about someone's lifestyle choices away in order to bring the salvation of Christ to a confused and searching soul.

When He finally arrives, blazing in beauty and all his angels with him, the Son of Man will take his place on his glorious throne. Then all the nations will be arranged before Him and He will sort the people out, much as a shepherd sorts out sheep and goats, putting sheep to his right and goats to His left. Then the King will say to those on the right, "Enter you who are blessed by my Father! Take what's coming to you in this kingdom. It's been ready for you since the world's foundation. And here's why:

> I was hungry and you fed me
> I was thirsty and you gave me a drink
> I was homeless and you gave me a room
> I was shivering and you gave me clothes
> I was sick and you stopped to visit
> I was in prison and you came to me
> (Matthew 25:31-40 MSG)

This is the mindset we must have personally. We must be others-focused in our daily lives, but how does this play out in the church. If we are to be others-focused in the church, we are going to have to adopt this mindset:

Think church-NOT clique.

In order for a church to grow, its people (especially leaders) must come to the realization that they are part of a church, not a clique. Now I know you are thinking to yourself, I am not involved in a clique. Are you sure? A clique by definition is a small and narrow exclusive group or circle of people. A church is also a group of people, but the church is supposed to be a large, inclusive, and diverse group of people. This means there is supposed to be people that are different than you in your church and you are to be pleased with it.

A common ideology says "I want some close friends to talk to, not some big church." What does God say? God wants us to have friendships and accountability. These things are great, but you can get that sort of thing through small groups or inviting people over to dinner. This atmosphere does not have to be your Sunday morning service. What is the mission of your Sunday service? Is it to get to know everyone like best friends or is to reach the lost? Is it to dive deep into worship music that unchurched guests don't understand or is it to introduce people to the Lord? What is the mission of the actual service? It's hard to know you have arrived at your destination if you didn't know where you were going from the start.

If we have this old ideology that you have to know everyone in the church really well, then you are making the church small and exclusive. You are taking it from a celebration of worship unto God and making it an invitation-only supper club. I have seen huge churches where there are still lots of personal relationships. If you are really honest with yourself, you don't know everyone as good as you wish you did already. You may be of the house church mindset, but if you live out *Invitality*, your house will soon be too small for the growth God brings.

Church growth is up to the people. The pastor can lead and should lead, but the people have to follow. A pastor can only invite so many people. In fact, the pastor is not the one out there every day in the harvest field of the workplace. The people have this distinct and awesome opportunity. A pastor alone cannot grow and sustain a church. As John Maxwell puts it "a leader without followers is just out for a lonely walk." If the people aren't friendly or open to others, the church isn't going to grow. A church is to be an "open" place. We are to live a lifestyle of inviting people in.

Have you ever noticed how standing in a circle with people makes you feel comfortable? Have you ever thought about how people may feel that are not in your circle? Everyone in the circle may feel good at that moment, but they are closed off to everyone outside? Next time you are at a high school football game look how many circles are around. No wonder teenagers always feel awkward and out of place. This is what people have done in their churches without even noticing. They like each other and have grown relationships with each other. They come to church and they stand in circles and they catch up with one another. But when a new person comes in the door all they see is a bunch of peoples' backs. Circles actually close new people out. This looks to outsiders like they don't fit into the clique. They may stick it out for one service, but you won't see them next week.

We are all the church and if you as an individual will adopt *Invitality*, it will catch on around you. Open your eyes to the people around you. Open your heart to their lives. Open up your church doors to them. Open up your circle of friends to them. In fact, always leave your circle open. Quit holding onto ideologies that keep others from feeling accepted and accepting Christ.

As a leader or as a believer you can actually hold your church captive from growth by keeping a clique attitude. I am not saying that you have to be best friends with everyone that walks in the door or with everyone that you invite. That is why we introduce people to others. We need to help people form relationships so that they can grow in Christ and feel comfortable even when we are not in the building. As Christians, we are to have a spirit of hospitality. Is your church run by a network of "good ol' boys?" People see that. Do people get a look if they accidentally sit in someone else's usual spot? Get over it!

Here is what I am trying to say. Think BIG church. Be open to others tactically by never closing a circle. You think this isn't a big deal, but body language is over 80% of communication. You are communicating all the time. Let's purposely communicate Invitality.

If you are insisting on having a personal relationship with your pastor, if you want to be able to come into his office at the spur of the moment, or if you want to be able to call him up all hours of the day for every problem, you are actually holding your pastor captive. You are holding his leadership captive. Now, a pastor is called to shepherd the flock. A pastor is called to ensure care for the people of God. I get that and I am on board. However, since God has called us to reach more people, we have to understand that the pastor only has so many hours in the day. There will come a day when the pastor cannot care for everyone. We must be willing to meet with other leaders that pastor puts in place. We must be willing to receive care from other leaders. We must be willing to share the pastor with other people and not hoard him/her to ourselves. Think church- not clique.

This is always the toughest for people who have had a personal relationship with a pastor because you have to learn to let go and let God take over. This doesn't mean that you can no longer ever meet with your pastor. It means that you will need to call and make an appointment. It's not really a big deal, if you will get past your old mindsets. Think about this. Any successful person makes appointments- even with their friends. Have you ever had to make an appointment called a tee time to go golfing with a friend? Your pastor isn't leaving you or your life, but things change. In fact, last week I had a congregant call and make an appointment with me to go golfing. You can do more ministry than you think in a round of golf.

I know that we all adapt to change differently, but what are you going to do? Are you going to tell God that He can't reach more people and that you don't want part in His plan? Are you going to deny reality and move to a small church? What are you going to do when that one gets a revelation of the great commission? Are you going to church hop again? You want the church to welcome your friends that you reach, so please welcome all people's friends that are reached.

Please treasure all the good times that you have had with your pastor. These are not taken away from you. Treasure the relationship you have built, but allow God to use your pastor to grow the church. If you won't let your pastor be a pastor of a bigger church, then you are stopping *Invitality* from working its work. If your pastor has grown the ministry to this point and the people hold him captive, God will take him somewhere that will allow him to reach the lost. Then, you won't have your pastor at all. Change is difficult on the pastor too, but we must all change our mindsets for the sake of the kingdom.

Invitality opens the doors of the church to all. This enables the church to fulfill its destiny in God. I love what Kenneth Hagin said in 2007-"Destiny is a matter of choice, not of chance" (Hagin, 2007). What will you choose for your church? Will you choose to have an open party for all or a members-only guest list? I find it interesting that after the first sermon ever preached by Peter, when the church was birthed, at least 3000 people give their hearts to Christ. Remember they understood all sorts of different languages. This means that God wants the church open to all sorts of people from all sorts of backgrounds.

Now, by personality, I am the type of person who likes to throw a party and invite all sorts of people. I look for reasons to party! I recently found out I am 3/16 Irish. That was reason enough to celebrate St. Patrick's Day. Of course, I celebrate it in a Christian way with tons of house guests that are not out of control. My wife, on the other hand, likes a more intimate style party with just a few folks to whom we can talk. This is how we are by personality and we balance each other out pretty well. But when it comes to the church of Jesus Christ, it is not a matter of personality. Jesus said that we are to go into all the world and preach that gospel to EVERY creature. ALL who believe and are baptized will be saved. He said that he wishes for all men to be saved and come to the knowledge of the Son of God. This doesn't give any room for something small, closed off, and exclusive.

Remember Luke 14:23 "Go and compel them to come in that my house may be full!" If the house of God is to be full, we need to choose to adopt attitudes that allow it to be full. This means that we put our personalities aside and adopt Jesus' spirit of hospitality. This means we choose corporately and individually to live out *Invitality*.

I remember Joe's story. Joe worked in customer service. He would always ask John (a church member) about why he was so happy. Then John would open up to him about Christ and spend a lot of time listening. One day, as John was reading the Bible in the break room, Joe came up to him, sat down, and directly asked him what he believed in. Joe testified of God's goodness in his life since accepting Christ. Over the next year, Joe was invited to church several times. He was told that the church was non-judgmental and would accept him in love. Joe usually worked Sundays, so John invited him to a book study. Once he found a service that he could attend, he came a few times, and received salvation. Now, Joe takes the time to go to John and tell him "thank you" for the invitation to church. He is experiencing the love of God and the people of the church have made a difference in his life.

Become a fan of your local church and of Jesus Christ.

> Then the master said to the servant, 'Go out into the highways and hedges, and <u>compel</u> *them* to come in, that my house may be filled. (Luke 14:23)

The word *compel* means to invite. Oftentimes, we think of inviting someone and it comes out like "Hey, I go to this church that's really excited about God and you're welcome to come with me if you want. You don't have to. It's up to you, whatever." This is an example of how we think of inviting people to something. Has Christ been good to you or what? Jesus is the best thing that's ever happened to us. What kind of sorry invite is that?

I was at an Iowa State University football game a couple of years ago and was super excited for the victory that we had just won over the University of Iowa Hawkeyes. People were storming the field and everyone was singing a song. It was an epic moment for my friend Josh and I. The problem was I couldn't let out a scream. I knew that I had to preach the next day. I made this mistake in the past and learned my lesson. I love people and don't want to make them listen to a bad voice for a whole sermon. I was so excited about my team at that moment, so you know what I did? I clapped what seemed like 500 miles per hour and I jumped up and down. I hugged my friend...while jumping up and down. When you're excited about something, you talk about it; you show it in your actions and your lifestyle and everything. I was excited and I wasn't holding back.

When we're excited about Christ, we show it in our actions and in our words. When we're excited about being a part of a church – a church that has vitality to it- we even show it in what we wear. Like a sports team that you love, be a fan! We've got the life of the Spirit of Christ Jesus inside us and we have a church that is full of life. That's a whole bunch of good. People need good in this life! So when we're inviting people into our lives and into our church, it shouldn't be impersonal and boring. It shouldn't be noncommittal and wishy-washy.

Inviting someone should not be like an impersonal mass mailer or a business card left on a table. If you want to waste paper and get minimal results just leave an invite on a table and hope that someone eventually walks through the doors of the church. If you are a fan of a team, you bleed the colors of your team. You wear team colors and talk with people about it. You don't just leave a team business card that says "come be a fan of my team." If you do leave something, you only leave it after a personal conversation.

A church invitation is a good thing. A church business card is a good thing. These are no substitutes for a fan of the church stepping out and saying, "Hey, Jack (use their first name), I don't know if you have off work on Sundays, but if you are I would love for you to come check out my church with me. What are you doing this Sunday?" Tell them some great things you enjoy about the church that are relevant to them. Tell them about the kid's ministry and about the worship music. Tell them about a small group they may fit well into or something. Then, give them the invitation card. Tell them "I know new places can be daunting so I will meet you at the front door at 5 minutes till 11 to help get the kids checked in to their classes. Does that sound good?"

God's word says, "Compel them." Compel them to come in. Let me remind you what compel means? It means to urge or to drag.

Did you ever have a good friend that invited you to church, and you were like, "I don't know if I want to go." But they were like, "Come on, man. Check out my church. You got to. You need to. It's awesome." You know what they were doing? They were dragging you by the Holy Spirit to church. They were doing this because they love you more than they love themselves. Do you think it made them comfortable to step out of their own personality and drag you to church? Do you think they wanted to babysit you? Do you think they just loved to spend extra gas money to pick you up because they didn't have any other use for their money? No! They loved you and cared about you. They cared about your eternal destiny.

As you are reading this today, think about who invited you to church and to Christ. Who was it that invited you into his/her life? Who was living as a fan and was willing to share the team? The reason you're in Christ is because someone loved you enough to get out beyond their own personality traits and out beyond their own lifestyle and out beyond their own habits and their own busyness and invite you because they cared about you. They cared about Jesus loving you. They loved you and that's why they invited you in. That's so cool!

Put this book down and call them. Or if you know that you will see them soon, go up to them and give them a hi-five or something or give them a fist bump. Thank them because they showed the love of God to you through Invitality.

Compel means to urge, drag, constrain. It means to herd up, to secure, and to bring about to a course of action. So you herd up a group of people. I am serious. Just herd them up. Speak out and say, "All you, come here. We're going to church on Sunday." Then you will hear excuse one as someone says they have to take care of personal business. Next, excuse two – I need to spend time with my special someone. Or excuse three – work. They're bringing all these excuses. Don't think they won't. They brought excuses to Jesus and we are doing his work on earth.

That is when you say, "No. You have got to come. You've got to check this out with me. You've got to see this. You've got to come experience this church. The presence of God is there. It's been great to me. It's been great to my life. Even if you don't accept Jesus, just come to my church. Just come with me. Come experience it. See what it's all about. Come on." Now that's compelling.

How are you compelled to eat? You sense hunger. I remember the September 12th when the restaurant Texas Roadhouse opened its doors in my hometown. My friend Philip was about to camp out overnight to get in and get their steak. I talked him out of it by hosting our leadership team meeting at the restaurant. I love a good steak. I can even go into that place not hungry, but when the aroma hits me something turns on. My body is like "oh yeah baby...let's eat." You really don't have to compel me too much when I smell the aroma of a good steak. There's an aroma – a savory aroma – in the air. Do you realize that we have the savory aroma of Jesus Christ and salvation with us everywhere we go?

> For <u>we are to God the fragrance of Christ among those who are being saved</u> and among those who are perishing. To the one we are the aroma of death leading to death and <u>to the other the aroma of life leading to life</u>. And who is sufficient for these things? (2 Corinthians 2:15-16)

When we're living in the blessing of God and in relationship with Jesus, we are releasing an aroma more savory than steak. You don't always have to say too much. They're already sensing it. They already see that you are happy. They have watched your life over the last few months and know that you are different. They don't know why, but they are hungry for whatever it is that you have. It doesn't take all the proper words, just a little invitation to experience the savory flavor of God. Share the meal.

Many times we think of evangelism in a box, but modern evangelism is not "Bible-beating" someone. Here is what I mean by "Bible-beating." It is not shoving the Word of God on someone who is not interested in listening. It's not shoving your agenda on them and causing arguments. That actually makes things worse for the people who have been praying for that lost person and showing them love. There are many ways to evangelize, but all of them should be in love. This book is focused on living a lifestyle of invitation. We must invite people into our lives so they can see the goodness of God.

Remember 80-90% of people that come to a church come not because of a sign, or a website, but because people invited them. According to statistics, 86% of the people who receive Jesus Christ do so because of a relationship with an individual. There's a total correlation there. It's personal, people. It's personal.

Someone most likely invited you. They invited you into their life. They invited you to a church, and by doing so, they invited you into God's church. They invited you to know His love. Thank God for that person. That person may not live in the community anymore. That person may be passed away now. That person may live in another community or go to another church. Thank God for that person. Now it's time for us to turn that around and become that person. Become a fan!

What is your Sunday tradition? If your Sunday tradition is like most church-goers it would be this. Get up, get dressed, read the paper, eat breakfast, get in the car at the last minute and get to church right as the first song is playing. How about sitting down with your whole family and becoming a family of Invitality? How about becoming fans of the Lord and the church together? Sit down with all of them and say that we are going to adopt a new culture into our family. God has called us to tell other people how good Jesus is and help them get to heaven. From now on, as a family, we are going to try to never go to church by ourselves. We are going to change our Sunday tradition to be more godly because we are godly. From now on, I will ask every Saturday night before bed "who are we picking up on the way to church in the morning?" After several weeks, this is how we could possibly sound. "This is a weird week family because we don't have anybody to pick up this week. We need some new people. We've taken everybody." Let's pray together for the lost and then share the goodness of God with others. Let's continue to be fans.

If you are going to be successful right away with inviting others into your life and into Christ, you must build margin into your life. What do I mean by that? A margin in this case deals with your time. People who are successful in evangelism look at their calendar, their daily agendas, and their items of things to do, and they purposely decide within their hearts that God is the priority for their day. Since they set God as priority as much as their personal to-do list, they build time into their schedules to leave room for an opportunity to share with someone. They purposefully build in margin.

If you're self-employed, glory! You have the ability to build margin into your day immediately. As soon as you do God will begin to show you opportunities to share. Let me say this about your career. Once the enemy of your soul knows that he cannot keep you from working, he is going to try to make work the focus of your life. He takes everything to the extreme. He's going to try to get you so focused on work that you're busy, busy, busy. If not careful you will be too busy and forget about building in extra time to share with others the goodness of God.

Then, all you think about – if you're self-employed- is the massive list of things you need to get done by the end of the day. Here is the problem. The enemy sees to it that at the end of the day you come home with more items on the list then you even began the day with. What do you do now? You decide to get up for an early start to the next day. It's a vicious cycle of to-do lists that are never ending. The enemy gets you so focused on the bills, the work orders, the time sheets, and meeting with clients that you forget the real work God has called you to: Invitality.

Don't fall into the trap of the enemy. Don't try to keep up with the schedule this world has you on. You are not of this world. You are of heaven and of the Kingdom of God and you are on a mission from God to reach people. I want to encourage you to build margin into your life. When you go into the grocery store, when you go to get the car worked on, when you go into the park– whatever you're doing- plan to take some extra time. If you're too busy to stop and share your faith, then you are being busy, but not fruitful. We want fruitful!

I steward some rental property and my tendency used to be to rush in and rush out any time I had to fix something. Now, I am changed. I remember a couple years ago when this change took place in me and I was visiting the property for some upkeep. Here is what happened. I simply asked the renter "how are things going lately?" The renter said "Aw, man, they're horrible lately." Next, there came a few cuss words. Now, I could have said nothing, left, and went home for dinner because that is what my flesh wanted to do. I could have been stunned by her cussing and turned off to the conversation. Instead, I realized that this moment is something I have prayed for and my time schedule has built in margin for moments just like this.

I have to insert this here. Just in case you didn't recognize it- this is a question that opens a door. I spoke in another chapter about a question to go fishing with. This one works great for me if I have already built a friendship with a person. I just say, "Hey, how are things going lately?" Often times, people just "spill their guts." Then I share with them about Jesus because I built the time into my schedule to do it. I ask them if they would like to receive him and I offer to pray with them or invite them to church. I do whichever I am led by the Holy Spirit to do at that moment.

In this case, I told the renter about how she was valuable. I told her God made her precious and valuable and not to put up with some jerk guy that is not going to treat her like God's princess. You should have seen the look on her face. It was like no one had ever told her she was precious. I would have said more about her value but I was there by myself and didn't want to put myself in an awkward moment with an emotional girl since I am married. I told her how Jesus can bring her peace and offered her Jesus. She said she used to go to church. Then, I invited her to my church. It was not 2 months before she came in the door with her daughter. She rededicated her life to God and her daughter gave her heart to Jesus for the first time. She had never attended a church in our city.

Here is another example of how one person from our congregation has applied the tactic of margin. This member of our congregation will go into her retail job two hours early sometimes, go to the break-room, sit down and read her Bible or another spiritual book. It is a break-room and she is just relaxing off the clock. She does it ahead of her shift so that she can be mentally ready and spiritually built up for her shift when it starts. Some customers are mean and rude to her at work, but this gets her ready for the shift. She says that there are many days she can't even get into her reading because God has other plans. Coworkers tend to come into the break-room and just begin to ask her questions. They start the conversation and she just begins to invite them into her life, to church, and to Christ.

One person named Pat came and would whisper questions to her so that co-workers wouldn't hear. He was especially shy. After sharing several times, she finally asked Pat "Do you know what it is like to go into a loving church, be caught up in awesome worship, and experience the Bible taught so you can understand it?" Pat thought about it and then admitted that he had no idea what that would be like. After about a dozen invitations, Pat came to a testimony potluck dinner. At the end of the dinner, Pat prayed and received Jesus as his Savior and afterward told the people at the table. He was crying when he came up to me and told me "thank you" for the awesome night. He received salvation that night, became a regular church attendee, and then a member of the church. To see the joy beaming from his eyes now is just amazing. He is growing in God!

This message means nothing if you don't apply it.

You need to figure out where your margin can be. Schedule it and watch God work! We must purposely build room in our daily schedule for the sharing of the good news. I know that we want to schedule meetings back to back to back. I know that we want to be productive, but don't you think that God will make up the difference? Try starting with a half an hour a day built-in with no plan but to ask someone a question and look for an opportunity. Be careful. It's addictive and fun.

10

Tactful—Not Tacky

This is important to understand as we move forward. *Invitality* is not crazy-ism. It's boldness, not loudness. It's loving- not judging. It's guiding, not pushing. Jesus was bold, but always purposeful and led by the Holy Spirit. He walked in Holy Spirit tact. He was labeled as an extremist by religious folk, but the people who didn't know God loved Him. They loved Him.

So relax and don't worry about trying to make me happy. Don't worry about living for the approval of your pastor. Change your life to be bold- not loud, to loving-not judging, to guide-not push people to Jesus. You only live for the approval of One and you don't see Him with your physical eyes.

I want you to understand that we are to be greeters for the kingdom of Heaven. I think of a greeter on Sunday morning at church. They're like, "Welcome to our church. Do you have any questions? Here's a bulletin, here's how things are going to work today, and this is what it's all about."

That's how we're supposed to be with the Kingdom of God. We are simply hosts or greeters into the Kingdom of God. Have you ever seen a greeter or host when you go into a restaurant that has absolutely no personality or tact? They stare at the little guest book and barely look up at you. Then in a gruff and robotic tone that makes you think you walked in the door right before closing, they mutter "How many?" It doesn't make you too excited.

We're to be greeters to the Kingdom of God. We are greeters to the things of God. Our words and the way we act open or close opportunities for people to experience salvation. Don't go into work and talk like this. "I *have* to go to church this weekend and work changing diapers in the nursery…ugh. Then, I *have* to pay my tithes. I know I am going to feel pressure to *have* to tell people about Jesus. God might heal me. Do you want some of what I have?"

This makes me sick that people would treat the riches of God's goodness with disdain. We are to live as greeters to the Kingdom of God! We are not hosts to some greasy fast food joint. We are the gatekeepers to the Kingdom of heaven. We have the ability to share with others and get God's resources and ability working in their lives for their good. Wow! What a responsibility and what an honor.

> Jesus sent His twelve harvest hands with this charge: Don't begin by traveling to some far off place to convert unbelievers. Don't try to be dramatic by tackling some enemy. Go to the lost, confused people right here in the neighborhood. Tell them that the kingdom is here. Bring health to the sick, raise the dead, touch the untouchables, kick out demons. You've been treated generously,

so live generously. Don't think you have to put on a fundraising campaign before you start. You don't need a lot of equipment; you are the equipment. (Matthew 10 MSG)

You are the equipment! You! Each and every believer is the harvest equipment that God wants to use. Remember earlier in the book how we talked about each person being an individual harvester. God says you are the equipment. When you think about what brought you to Christ, at some point you are going to find that a person shared with you the gospel. They were your harvesting equipment that reached you. They were the instrument of God. They were acting as a sharp harvesting instrument of God- a sickle. They weren't perfect, but they introduced you to a lifestyle where there is peace and joy, where your sin is taken away, where you can have a relationship with Jesus, the one and only Christ, and where you can have fellowship with your Creator. That's pretty awesome. In order to be a sharp and effective harvesting instrument for God we must be tactful in our communication.

A person that's really living a lifestyle of Invitality is led by the Holy Spirit.

They are tactful. They're bold, not brash. They walk in gentleness. They walk in meekness. Meekness is not weakness. Jesus is not weak. Meekness is a fruit of the Holy Spirit. We see this in Galatians.

> But even if you should suffer for righteousness' sake, *you are* blessed. "And do not be afraid of their threats, nor be troubled." But sanctify the Lord

God in your hearts, and always *be* ready to *give* a defense to everyone who asks you a reason for the hope that is in you, <u>with meekness</u> and fear; having a good conscience, that when they defame you as evildoers, those who revile your good conduct in Christ may be ashamed (I Peter 3:14-16).

Meekness means power under perfect control. By definition, you can't walk in meekness unless you have power to begin with (Vines, 2013). If you don't have any power, you are just weak. God wants us to have power and use it with meekness. The Bible tells us that we have been given a spirit of power.

For God has not given us a spirit of fear, but of power and of love and of a sound mind. (2 Timothy 1:7)

When you become a believer in Jesus Christ you are given a spirit of power. That power can be increased as well. We will go into this later in the book. For now, please understand that with great power comes great responsibility. We must live and share with meekness. In regards to sharing with others, this looks like a person who is courteous and not rude. It looks like the description of love found in I Corinthians 13. It looks like living with tact.

Tactful means to be considerate; perceptive; discreet, showing skill and sensitivity; having a sense of what is fitting for dealing with others; showing concern for others feelings; diplomatic; thoughtful (Merriam-Webster, 2013). Being tactful means we listen more than we talk. Let's listen more than we talk because when you ask a question, and they begin to answer, they're opening their hearts and their minds to you. That's when you know how to share the truth of Jesus with them.

Listening more than you talk helps you be cognizant of boundaries. If you're tactful, be cognizant. Is the person that you are talking to at work and on the clock? Are you trying to minister to someone and they're "on the clock?" Are you robbing work-time from their boss so you can pray with them? Or, are you "on the clock" and supposed to be working, but you are ministering to someone? Have you asked your boss if you're free to preach when you're working? I am, but my employment is different than most. If they're paying you to be a roofer, and you're on break-time, that's your time. But if they're paying you to hammer shingles, you get up there and you hammer with all the glory God gives you. If you can hammer and you want to talk and listen at the same time, then praise God. But I'm telling you, be cognizant about boundaries. Be tactful. Because you can be ruining your witness with your boss while trying to get a coworker saved. We need to walk in Holy Spirit tact.

Holy Spirit tact means that you are relevant to the situation. What do I mean by that? Here is an example. A while back I went over to a thrift store trying to find clothing for a costume party. It was a "dance of the decades" party for teens. A person gets to dress up in clothes from a decade. You could dress 80's or 60's or whatever. After what happened in the store, I just ended up with wearing an outfit from the 90's because I still have clothes in my house from when I went to high school.

So, I'm at this store shopping around through the aisles and I recognized somebody from the past. She's a lady that has zero tact. She comes up, and I say "hi" because I am courteous. Of course, you know I felt on the inside like yelling "run." Sometimes, I have a hard time letting go and distancing myself from people. In a matter of moments, she's there talking, and she is a loud talker. You know what I mean by a loud talker. No matter where she is and what she is talking about, her decibel level is above the norm. I notice that she is loud and so I look around and people are staring. Of course, the moment I look at the people staring they look away and stare elsewhere in the store.

She's talking about having a personal prophecy. She is talking super loud. She's talking about prophecy, and you know, I believe in prophecy. I believe God shows people things. But I also believe that people can get off in the ditch by seeking the spectacular and missing the supernatural right there in God's word. I remember that she went way beyond God's word years ago and that is why she couldn't handle my church anymore. If you are too smart for the Bible, you are getting over in the enemy's playground. The enemy couldn't keep her from the spirit gifts in God, so he took her over in a ditch on the complete other side of the road. I could see this is what happened as she talked, or, should I say, announced her prophecy in the store. She said God was calling her to go out on a boat and live on a boat and weird stuff. I know that God can ask us to do weird things according to this world sometimes, but her approach was awful and people were staring with awkward gazes.

And so, tactfully, I started to give her clues. I started to walk away and I started to talk to my daughters. I felt bad for my kids. I was trying to give her body language that says I'm a little uncomfortable right now. She could have easily said, "Hey, do you have a minute to talk?" I would have kindly answered "yes, outside." But instead, it went from hi to booya! She was just running me over with all this weird talk. I looked up, and I looked at one of the guys that was next to me shopping. He was giving me a smile and slowly nodding his head up and down with big eyes like, "Uh-hum. She's off her rocker." Do you understand this look? It's like you are nonverbally saying, "I hope you can get away. I hope that you can make it safely to the next aisle or to the dressing room, but you're on your own buddy. I care about your plight, but I'm not going over there. I'm not going closer to her."

I do not doubt that this lady has a relationship with God. I don't know. It's not my place. I'm not her pastor. It's not my place. One thing I can say is that she was irrelevant to the situation at hand. Instead of maybe drawing someone in where maybe we could have shared even in the store with other shoppers, it actually scared them away. You know how it is. None of us want to admit that we may be irrelevant or tacky at times. So I give you this charge to get secure in who you are in Christ and then go ask a friend for an unbiased opinion.

Find a friend and say, "Hey, I give you permission right now to be 100% bold with me. I will not hold it against you. Do I make people totally uncomfortable by the way I treat them in public? When I try to preach the Gospel and share my faith, am I just way off? Do people run from me?" The truth is you most likely don't know this is the case for you if you are irrelevant. The reason for this is that people start to run when you drive up to the house. They may mention something if you are not present in the room, but once you are there; they conveniently move towards the kitchen or find a distraction. Your friends are in the room before you get there and see the people run. You don't see people run. They've run before you've come.

I'm telling you – a lifestyle of *Invitality* is just being real. Did you have to run from somebody when you came to Christ? You should have been only running from the enemy and running to Christ. I imagine some people might have been running from the police when they accepted Christ. We ought not to be communicating our faith to others in such a way that causes them to run the other direction. They should be attracted to our tactful conversations. The only running they should be doing is running to Christ through prayer because of hearing the Truth. Don't discount the power of Holy Spirit tact. Walking with tactfulness doesn't change who you are, it just makes a way for you to bring who you are to the situation at hand without ruining opportunities. The Apostle Paul understood the importance of this.

> Even though I am a free man with no master, I have become a slave to all people to bring many to Christ. When I was with the Jews, I lived like a Jew to bring the Jews to Christ. When I was with those who follow the Jewish law, I too lived under that law. Even though I am not subject to the law, I did this so I could bring to Christ those who are under the law. When I am with the Gentiles who do not follow the Jewish law, I too live apart from that law so I can bring them to Christ. But I do not ignore the law of God; I obey the law of Christ.
>
> When I am with those who are weak, I share their weakness, for I want to bring the weak to Christ. Yes, I try to find common ground with everyone, doing everything I can to save some. I do everything to spread the Good News and share in its blessings. (I Corinthians 9:19-23)

This section of scripture does not mean Paul changed his convictions. Without violating biblical morality, he would go to great length to enter the world of others and lead them to salvation. It meant that Paul was perceptive to the situation- tactful- so that he did not offend people. If our communication style offends people it closes the door of communication. We want to be great communicators so that we can open doors, recognize opportunity, and seize opportunity to witness for Christ. We want to open our hearts and open our lives to others in a way that they can receive us. If they receive us, then we can open our mouths with gracious words. It's not enough to wear your Christian t-shirt. It's not enough to put a Jesus sticker on the back of your car. Those are great in showing that you are a fan of Christ. But if you are going around flipping people off, cutting people off, and bullying people with your God-conversation, that just makes them want to rear-end your car rather than ask questions about your bumper sticker. Our tactful style should open a door for our gracious words of salvation.

When was the last time someone who was not a Christian came over to your home to hang out? Invite them. If you are a tactful person, they will most likely say "yes." Open your life up. Quit being such a secret. This is one way you can create, look for, and seize opportunities to invite other people to Christ. Here's what I mean by create. Come up with some questions that work for you to get conversation started. Here is a list that you can draw from, but I want you to use your own if you can.

- Do you have a faith?
- What are you doing this weekend?
- Where do you go to church?
- (If they are new to work) How long have you lived in our town?
- (further into the conversation) Hey, when can you come to church with me?

I actually love it when they come over to my house and they start asking questions first. God seems to prepare people and I just give them what they are looking for. I love when they ask what I am doing for the weekend. When they ask me that, it always comes back to them something like this, "Oh, Friday, I'm doing softball, Saturday- family and football, but Sunday's all about church, baby!" I love my church. Being in my church is like the most powerful couple of hours I will have in my week. It energizes me and pumps me up. You want to go?" When they ask me a question, they open the door and I seize the opportunity.

As I mentioned earlier in the book, I steward some rental properties. One of the reasons I love to have these is because they help me to have contact with people who don't know Jesus. It's healthy for a Christian to spend time around non-Christian people. It helps us keep perspective on how good it is to have God in our lives. It keeps our focus from being inward all the time. I feel like sometimes people of a church think it would be great to work in a church because people don't cuss (or shouldn't) and the atmosphere would be healthy. The truth of the matter is we need to rejoice that God has made a way for us to get paid to be in our mission field. If you are mechanic, you are paid to bring people to Jesus there. If you are a salesman, you are paid to meet people's need for a Savior. If you are a business owner, you pay yourself to solve people's problems spiritually and naturally. What a gift to be in the workplace and be God's light there. I know that you need built up to stay going into work, but that is what your church is for. Someone called to bring Jesus to the workplace may be miserable working in a local church. That would be unhealthy.

So, I steward some rental property, and I was just done showing an apartment that was vacant and the prospective tenant and I were talking outside. We never used to do that, but now I have margin in my life. She asked when she could contact me to give me money for a deposit on the apartment. I said to the young lady, "Well, I have church in the morning, so I won't be able to receive a phone call at that point. But in the afternoon, I'll be able to receive a phone call." What's going on here? I just created an opportunity. If God then opens a further door in conversation and I hear Him say in my heart "pursue it," then I am ready. Let me explain.

Most of us don't think like that, but you can reprogram yourself. It's just being real. I just said, "Hey, I have church in the morning. I can't return phone calls during that time. But I'm definitely available in the afternoon." Then, in this case, she said, "Oh, where do you go to church?"

The door opened. Let me be absolutely clear that <u>the door opened</u>. Who opened the door? The Holy Spirit opened the door. How did he do it? I had margin to talk with a person and told her that I had church in the morning. This is like turning the door handle to open a door. Then, she opened the door for me to speak by asking a question. Did I have to wear a Christian t-shirt? Did I have to wear a tie? Did I have to pray in a special prayer language for fifteen minutes first? No. I just had to make myself available. That's it. I just made myself available, and I created that opportunity.

I seized the opportunity and told her about the awesome church I attend. I invited her to come to a service this Sunday and that I could save a seat right by my wife and me for her to sit in. She received the invitation with joy, but said this week would not work. I told her that she is getting a fresh start in a new place and that God has a purpose for her life. She said she would like to attend and check it out. I told her that I was going to take her at her word and I appreciated the conversation. About two months later she walked through the door with her son. I didn't know that she was also related to a church member who had been praying for this young lady for years.

When we are tactful we can recognize and seize opportunities to invite people in.

Here are some other ideas that may help you create opportunities to invite people. How many of you have an office and/or desk? Place something on your desk on purpose to start up conversation. Most people have a picture of their family on their desk. How about getting a picture of your family at some exciting even that your church is putting on? Here is what will happen. Someone will be sitting in your office and they will look at the picture and they will say "oh, is that your family?" They do not say this because they really wonder if that is your family. Do they think that you would take a picture of some random group of people enjoying life and put them on your desk? That would be hilarious. I could see myself doing that as a joke. They ask the question because they are trying to invite conversation. This is when you can say, "Yes this is my family and we had this picture taken at our awesome church. Where do you take your family to church?" They may give you some random answer because they haven't gone since the last major holiday. You talk up your church, the people, and Jesus like a fan and then invite them THIS SUNDAY to go with you. Booya! God opens the door and you seize the opportunity.

We have opportunities to recognize and seize constantly if we will be on the lookout. Once you start to notice them, you get better and better at seizing them. You just have to be willing to try!

Let me tell you this account of a church member named Don. Don owns a construction style business and oftentimes works right along-side his employees. One day, Don fell off a second story roof and should have died. He actually fell over two stories and landed on top of the privacy fence in the yard. Ouch. He should have been split in half or dead, but he's alive and he's well. He attends our church. God saved his life and God is healing him up.

So here is an example of a tactful conversation Don has with people since the accident. He was showing one of his workers how he fell and the worker said, "Man, you're lucky to be alive." Now, most people would say, "Yes, I am." The worker opens a door by saying, "You're *lucky* to be alive," and we close the door with the statement "yes I am."

We are either ignorant of God's opening or we are not willing to take five minutes to explain to them how we don't believe in luck. It could easily go like this and does for Don. He says something like "I know you think I'm lucky to be alive, but I believe that God saved my life. Do you know God? Do you have a relationship with Him? I don't do everything right, but I'd love to invite you to know God. He has changed my life. I would love to invite you to my church. In fact, what are you doing this Sunday? How about the next Sunday? You're working another job on Sundays? I didn't know that. Ok, well, we have this men's breakfast on Saturday mornings. Come with me. I'll buy your breakfast." The person would love a free breakfast.

How good are you at recognizing and seizing opportunity? Please understand that if someone asks you what you are doing over the weekend this is always an opportunity! Our answer should be like this "Well, I know I'm doing this and this, but the biggest thing I'm doing this weekend is that I'm going to church on Sunday morning. I have an awesome church. Do you go to church somewhere? I want to invite you to my church? Come with me. I'll pick you up."

If we hear something like "Oh, I'm unsure of choosing this apartment because of the school district. I have two kids and I'm kind of unsure of this area." That's just an open door. Do you see it?

Here is your answer: "I don't know much about the area, but I can tell you this. I have a good church that loves kids on Sundays, and whether you live here or not, you can bring your kids out on Sundays, and they will experience the love of God."

> *When it comes to open doors, we have to look for them and recognize them.*

When I show apartments, I try not to tell people that I am a minister. I don't hide it or anything, but I let them open up their lives to me first. If they know that you are professional Bible person, they change their words and you don't get the real individual. God wants reality. Here is another opportunity that I seized. I was showing this apartment to another single mom (Where are the real men in our society?). Anyways, she said she went to church in North Carolina, but she was afraid to go to any church here because she didn't know if people would judge her. Anybody ever heard that before?

I just said, "Oh man, I'm sorry you feel like that. I want to tell you my church will not judge you. Our church is full of love. Nobody's perfect. Come on. Come out. I want you to come. I want you to experience this. It's about love, not condemnation."

Do we recognize these open doors when they come to us? It's one thing to create an opportunity, it's one thing to look for an opportunity, it's one thing to recognize an opportunity, but we must choose that we are going to seize the opportunity. I can put a candy bar out in front of you right now, but unless you came up, grabbed it, and ate it, you wouldn't get the enjoyment from it. You can recognize a need in someone's life, but unless you'll take the step to seize the opportunity to invite them into your life, into your church and eventually into a relationship with Christ, they're not going to get it.

We can't sit back and say, "Oh, someone else will invite them. Oh, they're a teenager. They'll live a long time. Someone else will eventually invite them. Maybe they'll find God in college." We can't say "They are too busy with work right now to enjoy church. Maybe someone will speak to them in the nursing home." Come on! What if everybody said that? When will we step up and be the instrument of God to these people? We are God's harvesting instrument. God uses people. He wants to use you and that is why He has you reading this. Don't just create opportunity. Recognize it and tactfully seize it!

11

Invitality Empowerment

> What society sees and calls monumental,
> God sees through and calls monstrous.
> God's Law and the Prophets climaxed in John;
> <u>Now it's all kingdom of God—the glad news and
> compelling invitation to every man and woman.</u>
> (Luke 16:15 MSG)

People will come up with all sorts of excuses not to witness for Christ, but if you want to do it, God will empower you to do it. Like the scripture above says, it's all about compelling invitation to every man and woman. A lot of people sit back, they hear the Bible, they go to church, they listen to sermons, and they wonder why nothing's happening in their lives. There's something they're missing. When you hear it, you have to do it, and then you have what it says. You can't hear it and then have what it says. You have to hear it and apply it to get the rewards promised.

In order to reach your full potential in God and be who He has created you to be, you've got to incorporate within your life a culture of invitation. You are made to help other people come into the Kingdom of God. It's not a personality thing. It's a new creation thing.

The Bible says in 2 Corinthians 5:17 that we have been made into new creatures, a new kind of being in Christ Jesus, our old nature, our sinful nature has passed away, and we received a new nature. We obtained a brand new nature. What does our new nature do? It invites people. I will share it again. The real you invites people. Your new nature invites people into your life and into the goodness of God. It invites people to your church. It invites people into a relationship with God so that they can fulfill their destinies. While you are helping other people start the journey into their destinies, you are fulfilling yours! That's pretty cool.

You used to wake up on Sunday morning and think to yourself "I wonder who is going to be at church today." Now, all week long you ask yourself "Who can I invite to church on Sunday?" Then, when Sunday comes, you make reminder phone calls and plan to arrive early to meet them at the door. Why would you do all this? So that people can receive Jesus!

As a believer in Christ Jesus, you have a propensity, a natural inclination, to invite people into your life. You have to purposefully close that off, make your personality an excuse, or let culture lull you into apathy if you are going to be ineffective with the Gospel. Instead of wasting away all of the good things you have in Christ Jesus just go with your new nature. Invite people into your life and into Christ. I know that you have hurts, pains, experiences that you can't figure out. We all do, but that doesn't change the Truth of the gospel. It's time to trust Jesus in the midst of the pain and get back to being you. You are the embodiment of Invitality.

You have a supernatural propensity to invite.

Let's say that I have a propensity to water my lawn. I go out there to my yard with a hose, stand there, and shoot water all over the yard over a matter of hours and hope that I have some success. I can reach most all of my plants with some water I think. What if all of the sudden a fire truck comes by and the firefighters see what I am doing and they decide to lend me a hand? They decide to replace my little watering hose with their fire hose. This changes everything! I am still watering the lawn, but I am reaching everywhere with much more ability. Because I am tactful, I am not killing my plants, but I have the power to reach every one of my plants with all the refreshing they need.

This example illustrates how the Holy Spirit can empower a believer to be a witness. You have a supernatural propensity to invite people to Christ as a believer, but God wants to give you a fire hose. God wants to give you supernatural power to be a witness at a whole different level. Now, I could have said "no" to the firefighters offering me a bigger hose and you can say "no" to God offering you empowerment. It doesn't change what you are called to do, it just makes you empowered to do what you are called to do better! Be a witness. You can achieve greater results, with greater power, and have greater potential for the Kingdom of God if you receive empowerment from the Holy Spirit.

It is not about Catholic, Presbyterian, Nondenominational, Assembly of God, Word of Faith, Evangelical Free, or Methodist. It is about what God promises in the Bible! In fact, I know people from all of these denominations that have received this empowerment. It is not something I, nor anyone, is forcing you to have. It's something you should explore like salvation and receive it when you are ready.

> "For John truly baptized with water, but you shall be baptized with the Holy Spirit not many days from now." Therefore, when they had come together, they asked Him, saying, "Lord, will You at this time restore the kingdom to Israel?" And He said to them, "It is not for you to know times or seasons which the Father has put in His own authority. But you shall receive power when the Holy Spirit has come upon you; and you shall be witnesses to Me in Jerusalem, and in all Judea and Samaria, and to the end of the earth. (Acts 1:5-8)

Look at this. It says, "You shall receive power when the Holy Spirit has come upon you. And you will be witnesses for me in Jerusalem, Judea, and in Samaria, and to the end of the earth."

You see Jesus was talking here to his disciples. Today, I am talking to disciples and say to you, you shall receive power. You will receive power to be a witness. You may be asking: "when do I receive power to be a witness?" My answer to you is you receive power- empowerment- when the Holy Spirit comes <u>upon</u> you. That is our scriptural precedent.

Holy Spirit empowerment makes a difference in your life. It makes you bolder to be who you are called to be in Christ. When you are born again receiving salvation you receive the Holy Spirit in you. Remember Jesus said, "I will be in him a well, and out of his belly shall flow rivers of living water." That is when you receive the Holy Spirit in you at salvation. This empowerment comes from receiving the Holy Spirit upon you. This empowerment is for you to be a witness. This doesn't make you someone scary, crazy, or brash. This empowerment makes you stronger and more able to invite people to Christ. Here is how I know.

Other than seeing this happen to a lot of people in my own life and ministry, we see this happen to Peter in the scripture. Remember, Peter believed in Jesus. He was the one who declared that He was the Son of God. Yet, even though he believed in Jesus, when trial came he denied Christ and ran from the situation. Peter had walked on water with Jesus!!! He saw miracles and had cast out demons. He believed, yet he struggled to stand up for the cause. This same Peter, after he received the Holy Spirit empowerment to be a witness, stood up and delivered the first ever sermon after Christ's ascension in front of all sorts of people who were questioning him. The Bible says in Acts chapter 2 that about three thousand people were added to the Kingdom of God that one day because of Peter standing up and witnessing for the kingdom of God. This is what happens when someone is empowered to be a witness. It does not make them into a pastor; it makes them into a powerful witness in whatever they are called to do in life.

If you are called to help people by fixing things and that has led you to be a mechanic, don't think God is going to automatically call you to be a preacher. That is a separate calling. He does that sometimes, but that is not what this is for. If you are a mechanic, the Holy Spirit upon you will enable you to be a better witness as a mechanic. Maybe your calling in life is to make money and be a giver so preachers can be sent. Receiving the Holy Spirit upon you doesn't change who you are, it just makes you able to be an even better witness while you are bringing in money for the kingdom! Acts chapter 2 records the initial instance in scripture where the people in the upper room praying were filled with the Holy Spirit by Him coming down upon them.

> When the Day of Pentecost had fully come, they were all with one accord in one place. 2 And suddenly there came a sound from heaven, as of a rushing mighty wind, and it filled the whole house where they were sitting. 3 Then there appeared to them divided tongues, as of fire, and *one* sat upon each of them. 4 And they were all filled with the Holy Spirit and began to speak with other tongues, as the Spirit gave them utterance. (Acts 2:1-4)

This was the first time in human history that the Holy Spirit was poured out this way for all believers to receive upon themselves. In the book of John, it is written that the disciples, except for Judas and Thomas the twin, were present in a room to receive the Holy Spirit <u>within</u> them after Christ rose from the dead and prior to His ascension. But none of the disciples had received empowerment for being witnesses until the Holy Spirit came <u>upon</u> them as is recorded in the book of Acts.

> And when He had said this, He breathed on *them,* and said to them, "Receive the Holy Spirit." (John 20:22)

I am not going to get into details too much. I will just say that the Holy Spirit comes into a person when they are saved. The Holy Spirit can come on a person to empower them to be a great witness as well! I have seen people receive both experiences at the same time. I have seen them as separate experiences. One thing for sure, the Holy Spirit makes a difference empowering you with boldness when you receive him upon you. I highly recommend it for all believers. In fact, in scripture, it is the expectation.

In the book of Acts, when they found out people received Christ, they would send apostles to minister to them and help them receive the empowerment of the Holy Spirit. When these people received empowerment, they spoke in other tongues.

While Peter was still speaking these words, the Holy Spirit fell upon all those who heard the word. And those of the circumcision who believed were astonished, as many as came with Peter, because the gift of the Holy Spirit had been poured out on the Gentiles also. For they heard them speak with tongues and magnify God. (Acts 10:44-46)

Notice here that the Bible says they received the gift of the Holy Spirit. Sometimes it is referred to this way. Other times it is referred to as the baptism of the Spirit, and other times it is referred to as being filled with the Spirit. In all the cases that someone in the Bible had this experience they received empowerment. The Bible also records these people speaking in a divine prayer language-tongues. Notice here that the Holy Spirit was poured out <u>on</u> the Gentiles, not in the Gentiles. Gentile just means non-Jew. Here is another instance of the same experience to receive the empowerment to witness.

And when Paul had laid hands on them, the Holy Spirit came upon them, and they spoke with tongues and prophesied. (Acts 19:6)

You may be asking yourself two things. One, why haven't I heard of this before? And two, how can I receive this power to be a witness? You may not have heard about this because people get divided about topics that they cannot explain through their own reasoning. However, people from all backgrounds in all sorts of churches have received this empowerment. I know of priests who have received this empowerment and pray in other tongues, but they have a set of messages they are to follow in their denomination and this is not one of those messages. I also know that some churches like to preach that this experience died with the twelve Apostles. The problem with this theory of disbelief is that at least

120 people experienced it originally, including the Apostles, and they went out and ministered to a whole bunch of believers. Then Paul went everywhere teaching, preaching, and sharing this experience after it happened to him as well and he wasn't one of the original twelve. Not only that, people all through the centuries have had the same experience in their own bedrooms, in congregational singing, in prayer meetings, and in prayer without anyone laying hands on them and praying for them. The gift is from God. Denominational lines won't stop it. They can only slow it down. It's not an American theory. It's a biblical promise! I am not here to get into a deep theological argument. I am here to help you live a lifestyle of Invitality to the max!

So, how do you receive this power from God? You receive it when the Holy Spirit comes upon you. It's free just like salvation and you receive it just the same. You believe it, ask God for it, thank Him for it, and He gives it. You start living empowered and you can also start praying in another heavenly language called tongues. Your prayer language is for you and God. It's not meant to go around town and speak it to other people. They will think you are a freak. They don't understand this language. Only God does. It's from His kingdom and it's meant to be used mainly between you and Him. We only use our tongues publicly when given permission from our pastor. I hope that your pastor follows biblical standards for order in the church. He is the leader of the church. And there are Biblical standards for both praying in other tongues and the Gift of Tongues (I Corinthians 12:10) for use in congregational encouragement. I don't want to get into all that in this book. Just know that you receive when the Holy Spirit comes upon you. I will share instructions to enjoy this experience later in the chapter.

There are many experiences you can receive from God through the Holy Spirit. Here are two experiences. You can receive salvation which gives you the Holy Spirit within, but you can also receive the baptism of the Holy Spirit, which is the Holy Spirit upon you. The first experience enables you to grow Godly character. The second fills you to the brim and overflowing with the Holy Spirit of God. This gives you empowerment to witness. It enables you to minister with power to others. You can receive both salvation and empowerment at the same time. I have seen this happen in one instance like in Acts chapter 2. I have also witnessed it happen on separate occasions like are found elsewhere in the book of Acts. There is much that can be said here, but the point is to receive salvation and empowerment to witness. They are both available. God is a giver! I love how cool God is!

Now when you receive the Holy Spirit upon you, you receive power, not weirdness! Some people get all bent out of shape about the things of God because they have witnessed weirdos. I am telling you that weirdness is just people. People can be weird sometimes. This is not weird. God is not weird. People are weird. I can go to a hockey game, football game, coffee shop, mall, or grocery store and find someone who is just a little weird. That is not because of God and don't blame it on Him. Let's look back at Acts for our example.

> "But you shall receive power when the Holy Spirit has come upon you; and you shall be witnesses to Me in Jerusalem, and in all Judea and Samaria, and to the end of the earth." (Acts 1:8)

Did anybody see weirdness in that? No. We have to admit people get weird. We all have our weird-isms. I can go to your house, just sit down, hang out for one day, and pick out something weird that you do. You can pick out like fifteen that I do, but that is just people.

For instance, I have two spots where I put my shoes. What's up with that? That's a little weird. I have a shoe spot by the door and it's a bucket. Then I have a shoe spot in my room. Well, why do I need two shoe spots? I don't need two shoe spots. It's just a weird-ism. The Holy Ghost didn't give me that. That's just me. I can't blame that on the Holy Spirit.

Sometimes people get their sense of reality from the internet. Please do not do that. That is weird. Get your sense of reality from scripture! In scripture, God said through Jesus that He wants to empower you. He wants to empower you to be a witness. He wants to give you full power to be a witness. He wants you living this Christian life at full throttle. He wants you empowered to live out this invitation culture. He wants to give you power- not weirdness.

He's not going to make you spike your hair up, look crazy, and live "out of control" for God. If you spike your hair, that's your choice. If you live "out of control," don't blame that on God. The Holy Spirit is a spirit of a sound mind. Maybe you're going to witness to people who spike their hair, but He's not going to call you to be something you're not. He's going to make you more of who you are and He's going to give you boldness to do it. He's going to give you boldness to invite people into your life. He will give you boldness to invite them to your church and boldness to invite them to a relationship with Christ.

The results that you experience will be in direct proportion to your boldness.

Boldness is not loudness. Boldness is an attitude of faith experienced through your actions and words. Every believer has the potential to exude boldness. Biblical boldness is defined as outspokenness, unreserved utterance, freedom of speech, frankness, candor, cheerful courage; the opposite of cowardice, timidity, and fear. In the scripture it denotes a divine enablement that comes to ordinary and unprofessional people exhibiting power and authority. It also refers to a clear presentation of the gospel without being ambiguous or unintelligible (Vines, 2013).

Godly boldness is not a natural personality. Some personalities are more loud and abrasive and people may say they are bold. I would define that as brash. This is not biblical boldness. Natural boldness is a decision to line your lips and actions up with your attitude of mind. Supernatural or godly boldness is a decision to line your lips and actions up with your faith and the Holy Spirit leading.

God doesn't call a personality type. He calls all types of people and gives them all the ability to be empowered with boldness to minister and witness for Him. The Holy Spirit coming upon you can actually help you clarify your communication of the gospel so that people can understand it better. This is much different than emotional excitement which generally causes a person to lose focus.

Boldness can be increased in the believer's life in several ways. You can tap into the Spirit of God on the inside of you. You can ask God for boldness. You can meditate on His Word and attributes. You can find out who you are by being *in Christ*. You can fellowship with other believers. You can spend time with Jesus in prayer. You can experience the working of God for yourself. You can even be emboldened through persecution. All these are scriptural ways to increase boldness, but there is an empowerment to be bold as a witness that comes when you receive the Holy Spirit upon you.

With the baptism of the Holy Spirit, there is greater potential for you to invite people to Christ. When you are full of the Spirit of God it is easier to be led by His promptings. So as a believer in Jesus Christ, with a commission to go and to tell and compel people about the Kingdom of God through invitation, why would you not want to live full? Why would you not want all the power you can have to tell people about Jesus?

Kaye was a teenager when she first heard the message of *Invitality* and started living it out. She heard this message through youth group and took it to heart. You have to understand that Kaye was not the type of person that you would see standing on a street corner and yelling to a crowd. Kaye was fun-loving and friendly, but not brash and outgoing like others. She loved to play the guitar and drums, but as far as using a microphone in front of people, you could bet that was going to be a "no thanks." She was a teenager with friends who had surrounded her life and whom she liked.

In Kaye's junior year of high school, she took the message of *Invitality* to heart. She had been inviting her circle of friends into her life since her freshman year, but now she realized there was more purpose to these friendships than spending time together. She realized that she was an instrument of God to bring salvation to their lives. As I mentioned before, Kaye would not call herself the out-going preacher type, but she really decided to open up her life and open up her youth group so that her friends could experience salvation through Jesus.

Kaye got bold and started inviting her friends. Now, remember that boldness is not loudness. She wasn't loud and obnoxious. She was bold. In other words, she was purposeful and frank and spoke with cheerful candor. She was experiencing a rocking youth group and a growing relationship with God and didn't want that to be a secret to those she had grown to care about. Over the course of Kaye's last two years of high school, she invited many friends and acquaintances to youth group. She knows of at least eight of her friends that accepted Christ and stayed in the group until they graduated. She knows of two others that accepted Christ, but did not stay in the group because the parents had ties to a denomination. This is at least ten students that accepted Christ and had their eternal destinies changed because of one humble, cheerful, friend who decided to change the way she thought about evangelism.

How did she do it? According to Kaye, a similar scenario played its way out many times in conversation. With Wednesday being the middle of the week for most students in America, people would come into class or across her path and a conversation would happen something like this:

> Friend: "ugh...I hate Wednesdays..."
>
> Kaye would boldly (not always loudly) interject into the conversation
>
> Kaye: "I love Wednesdays! They are my favorite day of the week!"
>
> Friend: "Why?"
>
> At this moment a door was opened for her to share and invite. She would say this:
>
> Kaye: "I love Wednesdays because I get to go to youth group. It's absolutely awesome and you should come with me. Will you go with me tonight at 7pm?"

Of course a few more questions about a youth group and church would come up, but each time she would bring it back to the main point of youth group being awesome and asking them to come with her this Wednesday at 7pm.

Just think of the exponential effect of those ten people giving their hearts to Christ. It started with Kaye then you had ten others. These are not just numbers. These are people. These are lives with friends, families, pains, hurts, and joys. Because of Kaye's *Invitality* Jose, Kassi, Jules, Nicki, Zac, Mirna and others received salvation. Now those can go, share, and make a difference. I can just imagine how when Kaye gets to heaven someone will come up to her and say "Hey Kaye, thanks for inviting Mirna to youth group and to Christ. Because of your willingness to invite her, she shared with me and our whole household received salvation." *Invitality* is exponential to the individual and thus to the whole church! God wants every believer empowered to be a witness with boldness.

I want you to understand that *Invitality* is easy. Our key area to share Jesus with others is in our sphere of friends, coworkers, and family members. Kaye didn't wake up one day and say "I am turning into an evangelist." She didn't even wake up and say "I am going to purpose to do evangelism." I know Kaye and she is not going to say much in the morning at all. Kate simply heard the message of *Invitality* and began to adopt it as a lifestyle. She invited people into her life, she invited them to youth group, and then at youth group they were invited to know Christ.

I'm not calling you to be a pastor. I'm just inviting you to be more of who you're called to be. If you're called to be in the military, be in the military. Be everything God called you to be and do it with His power. Do it with His boldness. If you're called to work the job, work the job, and be full of the Holy Spirit while you do it. Being empowered by God is the difference between trying to do a job with hand tools and trying to do a job with power tools. Hand tools get the job done most times, but power tools are so much better. God empowers believers with boldness to be a witness. All you have to do is believe and receive it.

Going back to the book of Acts chapter two, God showed His Spirit coming down upon them like fire. It wasn't physical fire, but it was like fire. It was like fire in the spirit realm. It lit them up with boldness to witness. It put fire in them to go out after the lost and hurting. It will enable you to go out after the lost and hurting. It will enable you to live out your new life culture of Invitality. Let the love of God rule in your hearts as you boldly reach people with the message of the gospel.

Here is how to receive the Holy Spirit upon you. Number one, relax. This is a gift so all you have to do is receive it and then speak. Number two, ask God for it. Say this if you want to, but the best prayer is always from your heart. "Father God, I understand that I can have the Holy Spirit upon me to empower me to be a witness for You. I want that. I want to be the best possible witness I can be. I know that you are a loving Father and want to give me this. Thank you. So right now I ask You to send the Holy Spirit to come upon me. I will receive the Holy Spirit upon me now and I will now speak with other tongues." Number three, the Holy Spirit is moving upon you now and will prompt your tongue with sounds and syllables that you won't understand. You need to be bold and speak them. As you do, the language will come more and more. The Holy Spirit gives the language, but you do the speaking. If you try to understand the language with your mind, it will stop the ability to speak. Number four; continue to pray in your prayer language by stopping and starting. This endowment of power is always with you now, but you can pray in tongues by choice. If you are feeling low on boldness someday pray in tongues and it will be like recharging your boldness battery.

Prayers that rock your world!

Salvation Prayer

"God in heaven, I believe that Jesus is the Christ, the Son of God. I believe that He came to earth and did miracles. I believe that He died for my sins and rose from the dead. You made Him over heaven and earth. Right now I declare Jesus as Lord and leader of my life. Thank you for saving me and being my heavenly Father. I pray this in Jesus name. Amen."

Prayer for Holy Spirit Empowerment

Father God, I understand that I can have the Holy Spirit upon me to empower me to be a witness for You. I want that. I want to be the best possible witness I can be. I know that you are a loving Father and want to give me this. Thank you. So right now I ask You to send the Holy Spirit to come upon me. I will receive the Holy Spirit upon me now and I will now speak with other tongues in Jesus name, Amen.

Invitality prayer

Father God, help me to embody Invitality today. I choose to open my life and my church up to others by asking questions and testifying. Is there someone in particular that you would like me to focus on today? Help me to recognize opportunity to share about your Kingdom. Lead me with the words to say and how to say them for the best results. Most importantly, empower me to seize the opportunities and pray with people to receive salvation. I pray in Jesus name, Amen.

A special invitation in case you missed it the first time!

Download the free *Invitality* Transformation Guide.

Go to: http://bit.ly/2zufQLF

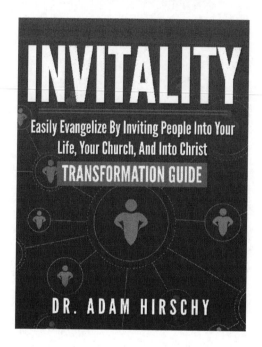

The *Invitality* Transformation Guide is a fast-start personal and small group life-change experience! You will grow spiritually and maximize results! When you download, you will enjoy full access to the *Invitality* community. The *Invitality* community is a group of world-changers sharing experiences, asking questions, praying, and encouraging one another!

Bibliography

The accounts within this book are factual and taken from personal interviews with people who have embraced *Invitality*. The author chooses to keep names of individuals within all the accounts because evangelism is personal. Only the names have been changed publication purposes.

Unless otherwise noted, all scripture quotations are from the New King James Version of the Bible.

Scripture quotations marked (AMP) are taken from The Amplified Bible, New Testament, Copyright © 1954, 1958, 1962, 1964, 1965, 1987 by The Lockman Foundation, La Habra, California.

Scripture quotations marked (NLT) are taken from Holy Bible. New Living Translation copyright© 1996, 2004, 2007 by Tyndale House Foundation. Used by permission of Tyndale House Publishers Inc., Carol Stream, Illinois 60188. All rights reserved.

Scripture quotations marked (MSG) are taken from The Message Copyright © 1993, 1994, 1995, 1996, 2000, 2001, 2002 by Eugene H. Peterson

Assisi, F. o. (2013, November 23). Retrieved from BrainyQuote.com: http://www.brainyquote.com/quotes/quotes/f/francisofa109569.html

Beamer, I. (2011). Intercultural Communication in the Global Workforce. New York: Mcgraw Hill.

Donovan, S. S. (2013). Retrieved from HUD.GOV U.S. Department of Housing and Urban Development: http://portal.hud.gove/hudportal/HUD?src=/topics/housing_choice_voucher_program_section_8

Hagin, K. (2007, February). Winter Bible Seminar. (K. Hagin, Performer) Rhema Bible Church, Broken Arrow, Oklahoma, USA.

Hayford, E. E. (2002). New Spirit Filled-Life Bible. Nashville, TN: Thomas Nelson, Inc.

lifewayresearch.com. (2006). Retrieved from LifeWay-Research: www.Lifewayresearch.com/

Mac, T. (2001, January 1). Get This Party Started. Momentum. Forefront Records.

Merriam-Webster. (2013, November). Retrieved from Merriam-Webster.com: http://www.merriam-webster.com/dictionary/invite

Merriam-Webster. (2013, November). Retrieved from Merriam-Webster.com: http://www.merriam-webster.com/dictionary/vitality

Merriam-Webster. (2013, November). Retrieved from merriam-webster.com: http://merriam-webster.com/dictionary/testify

Reiner, D.T. (2003). Ten Surprises about the Unchurched. Understanding their hearts and minds. Building Church Leaders. http://www.buildingchurchleaders.com/articles/2004/102704.html

Vines, W. (2013). Vine's Expository Dictionary of New Testament Words. Retrieved from Vine's Expository Dictionary of New Testament Words: http://www2.mf.no/bibel/vines.html

Wesley, J. (2013, November 23). Retrieved from Brainyquote.com: http://www.brainyquote.com/quotes/authors/j/john_wesley.htm

Can You Help? Two ways!

Thank You for Reading My Book!

1- I really appreciate all of your feedback, and I love hearing what you have to say. I need your input to make the next version of this book and my future books better. Please leave me an <u>honest review on Amazon</u> letting me know what you thought of the book.

2- Receive ministry updates and join our Support Team! Send the Gospel of Jesus Christ around the world, helping people love, live, and lead compelling!
Go to: <u>http://bit.ly/32hYXjl</u>

Thanks so much!
Dr. Adam Hirschy